2021

CALIFORNIA SUMMITS

Hiram Peak

Santa Ynez Mountains

CALIFORNIA SUMMITS

A GUIDE TO THE 50 BEST ACCESSIBLE PEAK EXPERIENCES IN THE GOLDEN STATE

Matt Johanson

FALCONGUIDES

GUILFORD, CONNECTICUT

FALCONGUIDES®

An imprint of Globe Pequot, the trade division of The Rowman & Littlefield Publishing Group, Inc.
4501 Forbes Blvd., Ste. 200
Lanham, MD 20706
www.GlobePequot.com

Falcon and FalconGuides are registered trademarks and Make Adventure Your Story is a
trademark of The Rowman & Littlefield Publishing Group, Inc.

Distributed by NATIONAL BOOK NETWORK

Copyright © 2021 The Rowman & Littlefield Publishing Group, Inc.

Photos by Matt Johanson

Maps by Trailhead Graphics, Inc.

British Library Cataloguing in Publication Information available

Library of Congress Cataloging-in-Publication Data

Names: Johanson, Matt, 1970- author.
Title: California summits : a guide to the 50 best accessible peak experiences in the Golden
    State / Matt Johanson.
Description: Guilford, Connecticut : FalconGuides, [2021] | Summary: "California Summits
    guides readers to 50 beautiful, attainable peak hikes. Hikers can summit most in a day,
    and sometimes in just a few hours, with a minimum of experience and gear. Everyone
    from families to experienced peak-baggers will find something to love. Hike up scenic
    Mount Tamalpais overlooking San Francisco Bay, Yosemite National Park's grand Clouds
    Rest with its incomparable view of Half Dome, and snowcapped Mount Shasta, the state's
    northern jewel, among others. Stunning color photography and detailed hike descriptions
    provide inspiration and information for hikers of all ages and experience levels"— Provided by
    publisher.
Identifiers: LCCN 2021010690 (print) | LCCN 2021010691 (ebook) | ISBN
    9781493048168 (paperback) | ISBN 9781493048175 (epub)
Subjects: LCSH: Hiking—California—Guidebooks. | Mountains—Recreational
    use—California—Guidebooks. | California—Guidebooks.
Classification: LCC GV199.42.C2 J64 2021 (print) | LCC GV199.42.C2
    (ebook) | DDC 796.5109794—dc23
LC record available at https://lccn.loc.gov/2021010690
LC ebook record available at https://lccn.loc.gov/2021010691

♾️™ The paper used in this publication meets the minimum requirements of American National
Standard for Information Sciences—Permanence of Paper for Printed Library Materials, ANSI/
NISO Z39.48-1992.

*For all those who stepped up to fight COVID-19, racism,
and California's wildfires in 2020 and beyond.*

High Sierra

CONTENTS

ACKNOWLEDGMENTS   xii

INTRODUCTION   xiii

PEAK FINDER   xix

Bay Area   *1*

1. Mount Davidson   5
2. Mount Diablo   9
3. San Bruno Mountain   13
4. Mount Tamalpais   17
5. Montara Mountain   21
6. Mission Peak   27
7. Hawkins Peak   31
8. Mount Umunhum   37
9. Mount Saint Helena   41
10. Mount Sizer   45

More Mountains in the Bay Area: Redwood Peak, Fremont Peak, Mount Livermore   50

SoCal   *55*

11. Mount Hollywood   59
12. Ryan Mountain   63
13. Echo Mountain   67
14. Montecito Peak   71
15. Butler Peak   75
16. Cuyamaca Peak   79
17. Mount Baden-Powell   85
18. Tahquitz Peak   89
19. San Jacinto Peak   93
20. Mount San Antonio   97

More Mountains in SoCal: Throop Peak, Sandstone Peak, Keller Peak   102

Sierra Nevada 107

21. Little Baldy — 111
22. Gaylor Peak — 115
23. Mount Judah — 119
24. The Watchtower — 123
25. North Dome — 127
26. Hiram Peak — 131
27. Granite Chief — 135
28. Jobs Peak — 139
29. Stanislaus Peak — 143
30. Mount Tallac — 149

More Mountains in the Sierra Nevada:
Sierra Buttes, Ellis Peak, Lookout Peak — 152

Eastside 157

31. Reversed Peak — 161
32. Tioga Peak — 165
33. Chocolate Mountain — 169
34. Wildrose Peak — 173
35. Mount Solomons — 177
36. Mount Starr — 181
37. Carson Peak — 185
38. White Mountain — 189
39. Lone Pine Peak — 195
40. Matterhorn Peak — 199

More Mountains in the Eastside: Dante Peak,
Trail Peak, Mount Gould — 204

North State 209

41. Goosenest — 213
42. Cinder Cone — 217
43. Black Butte — 221
44. Mount Eddy — 225
45. Castle Dome — 229
46. Lassen Peak — 233
47. Brokeoff Mountain — 237
48. Granite Peak — 241

49. Shastina   247

50. Mount Shasta   251

More Mountains in the North State: Herd Peak,
Gray Butte, Mount Bradley   258

AFTERWORD   261

HIKE INDEX   264

ABOUT THE AUTHOR   265

Overview

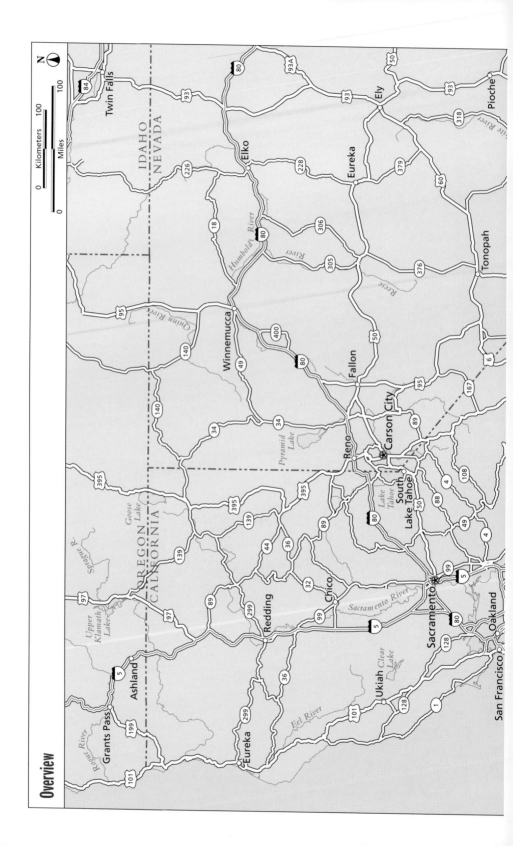

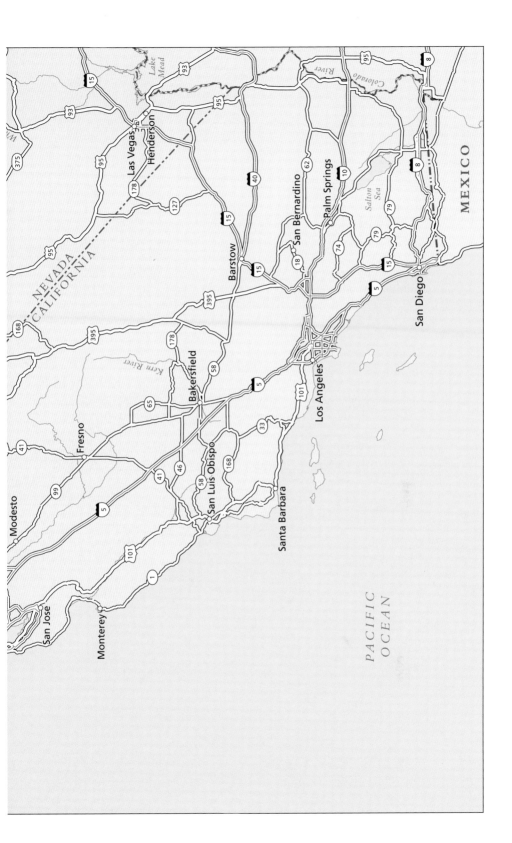

ACKNOWLEDGMENTS

Scaling the mountain of writing *California Summits* required the help of many climbing partners.

I'm grateful to Jess d'Arbonne, Melissa Baker, Joanna Beyer, Kristen Mellitt, Katie O'Dell, and others at Globe Pequot Press who believed in this project and helped me to see it through.

Thanks to the dozens of park rangers, forest employees, and other experts who fact-checked the manuscript, helping me to improve the book's accuracy and detail. Despite a pandemic and wildfire season that no doubt complicated their lives, they kindly volunteered their time to do so. They include Zach Alexander, Timothy Babalis, Craig Beck, Zachary Behrens, Jon Carney, Cindy Carrington, Ana Cholo, Sarah Clark, John Clearwater, Scott Clemons, Adam Collins-Torruella, Jan Cutts, Matthew Delcarlo, Christian Delich, Marty Dickes, Gavin Emmons, Mark Fincher, Joe Flannery, Diana Fredlund, Patrick Goodrich, Nancy Harmon, Lisa Herron, Patrick Joyce, Sintia Kawasaki-Yee, Paul Koehler, Don Lane, Maureen Lavelle, Ken Lavin, Don Lee, Duane Lyon, Miguel Macias, Kaitlin Mansfield, Dave Mason, Jean Nels, Alison Nielsen, Shanda Ochs, Rebecca Paterson, Christopher Pollock, Jacquie Proctor, Amelia Ryan, Carla Schoof, Madison Sink, Brandi Stewart, Elizabeth Storey, Kevin Turner, John Verhoeven, Lisa Wayne, Gordon Willey, and Andy Zdon.

Extra credit goes to these potent proofreaders from my journalism class at Castro Valley High School: Victoria Ceaser, Ada Chen, Austin Coffelt, Corinne Davidson, Olivia Dooley, Andrew Hui, Brinkley Johansen, Komal Khehra, Brooke Kundert, Cecilia Lin, Ali Nosseir, Paulina Peltola, Alex Tam, Alice Tang, Ethan To, and Amanda Wong. Way to go, great ones! Long live The Olympian Media Empire!

Others who provided advice, encouragement, and support include Liz Bowling, Kirsten Evers, Bill Gracie, Kory Hayden, Becky Moore, and Bubba Suess.

Most of all, thanks and love to my wife, Karen Johanson, and my entire family for supporting this effort and me.

INTRODUCTION

Raging wind shook our tent so fiercely that it felt like a high-elevation earthquake. Four of us camped in two tents at Helen Lake, about halfway up 14,179-foot Mount Shasta. But the screaming gale broke the poles of one tent, forcing all four of us to cram into the other. Sleep was impossible.

As dawn broke, we faced a decision: down or up? On our first big mountain climb, continuing the ascent made no sense. Wind blasted snow off the slopes above and felt strong enough to do the same to us. Choosing a flimsy tent wasn't our only rookie mistake, either. We wore too much cotton, brought insufficient sun protection, and had no experience using our rented crampons and ice axes. Most other climbers were wisely heading down.

But we pushed up anyway, as we were just too young and stubborn to descend without at least trying to continue. Hours of hard labor burned our thighs and our lungs. High-altitude sun scorched our faces beet red. Only youthful vigor, stubborn determination, and a healthy dose of beginners' luck let us muscle our way to the summit. Then the cold chased us back down minutes later.

Still, pulling off such a significant climb on our first try felt great. That adventure marked the beginning of my mountain climbing career. Hundreds of other summits followed over the next twenty-five years. A few favorites include Ryan Mountain, Matterhorn Peak, and Mount Tallac. Most presented challenges, like cold, heat, loose rock, route finding, and thin air, to name a few.

But the greater the hardship, the greater the payoff. Each of the peaks delivered rewarding summit views and emotional satisfaction. Climbing throughout the state over the years taught me about California's history, ecology, and geology. Most important, the adventures helped me bond and make memories with family and friends.

Between the coast and the desert, thousands of mountain experiences await climbers in the Golden State, and most are considerably easier than my first effort on the highest peak in Northern California. This guidebook presents a sampling in five major regions. Each section features outings with a variety of difficulty levels, starting with the easiest and building up to more challenging ones. Our collection focuses on ascents achievable in a single day without climbing gear. Most include only Class 1 terrain (walking on trails). Those with Class 2 (walking on rough territory) or Class 3 (scrambling using handholds and footholds) portions have only small amounts of off-trail travel.

Some may find curious the exclusion of two worthy and popular peaks: Half Dome and Mount Whitney. Both attract so many admirers that obtaining their required permits has become in some ways more challenging than their summit hikes. For that reason, I prefer to direct attention to other lesser-known but equally fulfilling adventures elsewhere.

Mount Shasta

But this author could not write a California mountain climbing guide without including Mount Shasta and its offshoot, Shastina. These two are the book's only outings that will require crampons and ice axes in typical conditions during summer and early fall. I have purposely listed them last to encourage readers to build up to them over time and attempt them with an abundance of ability and experience. In other words, I hope you arrive smarter and more prepared than I was in 1995.

Mount Shasta drew my attention again decades later as I climbed throughout California to research this book. The massive and magnificent volcano beckoned me as I

Ted and Tom Johanson ascended the north slope of Mount Shasta in 1969.

traveled in the North State, and I yearned to climb it again in better fashion than before. In addition, a family photo of my dad Tom and Uncle Ted standing happily on the summit in 1969 provided further inspiration. My brother Dan and cousins Andy and Peter joined me for a fiftieth anniversary climb in honor of our late dads and uncles who introduced us to outdoor pursuits.

Rising at four a.m., we strapped on our crampons and started up the steep Hotlum-Bolam Ridge. Hours passed, the sun rose, and the air got thinner as we got wearier. But enthusiasm and adrenaline increased as our goal got closer. When we turned a last corner and the summit block came into view, cautious optimism gave way to euphoria. The four of us regrouped to summit together, with Dad and Uncle Ted along in spirit.

Distant snowcapped peaks, green valleys, and scattered clouds filled an especially grand and rewarding view. More than that, our 2019 Mount Shasta ascent delivered warm camaraderie and deep family fellowship. Even before we summited, the climb had become my all-time favorite. Somewhere between my rookie attempt and its sequel a quarter-century later, I must have learned to value the journey as much as the destination. I still like reaching the summits, though.

I truly hope this book helps readers find as much happiness as I have from climbing California's mountains.

WEATHER

Weather varies widely in the nation's third-largest state consisting of more than 163,000 square miles. The Bay Area enjoys a mild climate, receiving only light and rare snowfall on its highest peaks in winter and occasionally reaching triple-digit temperatures in summer. Southern California is generally warmer, especially in its deserts, which have recorded the highest temperatures in US history. Although SoCal experiences moderate winters, it possesses higher mountains than the Bay Area, which accumulate more snow.

Fifty years after the Johanson brothers' climb, their sons and nephews re-created their adventure.

The Sierra Nevada contains the state's highest mountains and captures the majority of its snowfall, which closes high passes in winter and spring. Similarly, Northern California collects significant snow but also endures hot summers, especially in the upper Central Valley.

In the Bay Area and the lower peaks of SoCal, year-round climbing is possible. Elsewhere in the state, summer and fall provide the most favorable conditions for ascending peaks. However, the state's high country offers no guarantees concerning weather even in warm seasons. Rain, hail, and snow can fall on every day of the year. Afternoon thundershowers are common and lightning can be deadly. For this reason, starting early on longer routes improves prospects for successful outings. Some of this collection's climbs make wonderful winter adventures in the right conditions for those adept in cross-country skiing or snowshoeing.

Visitors can obtain weather information from the National Weather Service (weather .gov) and from park and forest websites, entrance stations, and visitor centers.

FLORA AND FAUNA

California hosts more than 7,000 species of plants, including many found nowhere else on Earth. Among hundreds of wildflower species blooming each spring is the California poppy, the state's official flower.

Rare trees that hikers can see on this book's outings include bristlecone pines (the world's oldest trees, which grow in the White Mountains Range), giant sequoias (the world's largest trees in the western Sierra), foxtail pines (at high elevations of the eastern and southern Sierra), and Joshua trees (in the Southern California desert).

Poison oak grows on some shorter peaks like Mount Diablo and Mount Sizer. Thankfully, it does not grow above 5,000 feet and poses no problem on most of our summit hikes. Still, hikers should learn to recognize the shrub that sprouts leaves of three. Leaves are green in spring and summer, red in fall, and fall off the plant in winter. Avoid touching any suspicious plant below 5,000 feet.

Protected and endangered species include Sierra bighorn sheep, bald eagles, and California condors, each of which has happily achieved population growth in recent years. Long extinct in California, gray wolves have recently migrated from other states in small numbers.

Black bears populate mountain areas. Though they do not attack people, they are a concern for campers and drivers. Yosemite, Lake Tahoe, and other communities have reduced human–bear conflicts by requiring food and trash storage in bear-proof containers. Drivers remain a problem, though, and automobile accidents threaten and kill both bears and people. Please protect bears by observing speed limits and by securing food and trash while staying in their habitats.

Mosquitoes pose an annoyance in spring and summer. They hatch first at low elevations and work their way up the mountains as snow melts. Their numbers are greatest near standing water. Many deal with these pesky bloodsuckers using nets and chemicals; long-sleeved shirts and long pants are helpful, too.

Last of our notable species, giardia has infected water sources and sickened visitors. To kill the microscopic parasite, officials recommend boiling water or treating it with iodine. Water at low elevations (especially beneath camping areas or livestock) is more likely to be infected than high-altitude snowmelt. Take the means to purify water and err on the side of caution.

RESTRICTIONS AND REGULATIONS

Most outings in this collection require no permit for day use, with a few exceptions, like Mount Shasta, Mount Tallac, and Tahquitz Peak. Those who wish to camp on federal lands need wilderness permits from park or forest offices. These are usually free, though some land agencies do charge a small fee for reservations.

A few distinctions between national forests and national parks are worth knowing. In forests, camping on undeveloped land is legal and a great way to go. Dogs are allowed and there are no entrance fees. Within national parks, visitors must camp in developed campgrounds or in the backcountry (with a permit). Dogs are legal only on leash and in developed areas. You'd better believe there are entrance fees.

In Southern California, parking at popular national forest trailheads requires an Adventure Pass, available through the Forest Service and at local retailers.

Mount Tallac

PEAK FINDER

- Family-Friendly outings are suitable for children ages 10 and older.
- Dog-Friendly hikes may have leash requirements.
- Bikeable outings may have different routes than the hiking directions and maps indicate.
- Winter-Worthy treks are suitable for those adept with snowshoes or cross-country skis, and may also have different routes than the suggested hikes.
- Free hikes have no required entrance, permit, or parking fees.
- High There summits exceed 10,000 feet.
- Could Be Campy outings are suitable for overnight trips, which could require wilderness permits.

Bay Area

SUMMIT	FAMILY-FRIENDLY	DOG-FRIENDLY	BIKEABLE	WINTER-WORTHY	FREE	HIGH THERE	COULD BE CAMPY
1. Mount Davidson	●	●		●	●		
2. Mount Diablo	●		●	●			
3. San Bruno Mountain	●		●	●			
4. Mount Tamalpais			●	●	●		
5. Montara Mountain				●			
6. Mission Peak		●	●	●	●		
7. Hawkins Peak				●			
8. Mount Umunhum			●	●	●		
9. Mount Saint Helena			●	●	●		
10. Mount Sizer			●				●
A. Redwood Peak	●	●		●	●		
B. Fremont Peak	●	●	●	●			
C. Mount Livermore	●			●			

SoCal

SUMMIT	FAMILY-FRIENDLY	DOG-FRIENDLY	BIKEABLE	WINTER-WORTHY	FREE	HIGH THERE	COULD BE CAMPY
11. Mount Hollywood	•	•		•	•		
12. Ryan Mountain	•			•			
13. Echo Mountain	•	•		•	•		
14. Montecito Peak		•	•	•	•		
15. Butler Peak		•	•		•		
16. Cuyamaca Peak		•		•			
17. Mount Baden-Powell		•		•			
18. Tahquitz Peak		•					•
19. San Jacinto Peak				•		•	•
20. Mount San Antonio		•		•		•	•
D. Throop Peak	•	•					
E. Sandstone Peak		•		•	•		
F. Keller Peak		•	•				

Sierra Nevada

SUMMIT	FAMILY-FRIENDLY	DOG-FRIENDLY	BIKEABLE	WINTER-WORTHY	FREE	HIGH THERE	COULD BE CAMPY
21. Little Baldy	•			•			
22. Gaylor Peak	•					•	
23. Mount Judah	•	•		•	•		
24. The Watchtower							•
25. North Dome							•
26. Hiram Peak		•			•		
27. Granite Chief		•			•		

SUMMIT	FAMILY-FRIENDLY	DOG-FRIENDLY	BIKEABLE	WINTER-WORTHY	FREE	HIGH THERE	COULD BE CAMPY
28. Jobs Peak		•			•	•	
29. Stanislaus Peak		•			•	•	
30. Mount Tallac		•		•	•		
G. Sierra Buttes					•		
H. Ellis Peak		•	•		•		
I. Lookout Peak							•

Eastside

SUMMIT	FAMILY-FRIENDLY	DOG-FRIENDLY	BIKEABLE	WINTER-WORTHY	FREE	HIGH THERE	COULD BE CAMPY
31. Reversed Peak		•		•	•		
32. Tioga Peak		•			•	•	
33. Chocolate Mountain		•		•	•		
34. Wildrose Peak				•			
35. Mount Solomons						•	•
36. Mount Starr		•			•	•	
37. Carson Peak		•		•	•		
38. White Mountain		•	•		•	•	•
39. Lone Pine Peak		•			•	•	•
40. Matterhorn Peak		•			•	•	•
J. Dante Peak	•						
K. Trail Peak		•			•		
L. Mount Gould		•			•		

North State

SUMMIT	FAMILY-FRIENDLY	DOG-FRIENDLY	BIKEABLE	WINTER-WORTHY	FREE	HIGH THERE	COULD BE CAMPY
41. Goosenest		●			●		
42. Cinder Cone	●						
43. Black Butte		●		●	●		
44. Mount Eddy		●			●		
45. Castle Dome				●			
46. Lassen Peak				●		●	
47. Brokeoff Mountain				●		●	
48. Granite Peak		●			●		
49. Shastina				●		●	●
50. Mount Shasta				●		●	●
M. Herd Peak	●	●	●	●	●		
N. Gray Butte	●	●			●		
O. Mount Bradley		●		●	●		

Map Legend

Transportation

═(5)═	Interstate Highway
═(40)═	US Highway
═(89)═	State Highway
═══	County/Forest Road
====	Unpaved Road
------	Featured Trail
------	Trail or Fire Road
....	Off Trail Hike
•—•—•	Tram
—┼—┼—	Ski Lift

Water Features

⬭	Body of Water
∿	River/Creek
∿	Intermittent Creek
≋	Waterfall
⌀	Spring

Symbols

(1)	Trailhead
▲	Mountain/Peak
🏠	Ranger Station
❓	Visitor Center
🎿	Ski Area
■	Point of Interest
P	Parking
⛱	Picnic Area
▲	Campround
🗼	Tower
◐	Overlook

Land Management

▭	National Park/Forest
▭	Wilderness Area
▭	State/Local Park

Golden Gate Bridge

Mount Diablo

BAY AREA

Cold air and clouds blanketed Mount Umunhum in the early hours of September 14, 2017, but temperatures soon warmed to match the hearts of the mountain's people. Restricted for decades while the US military used it for a Cold War–era radar base, the "Place of the Hummingbird" welcomed back Native Americans for their first ceremony in more than 200 years.

Members of the Amah Mutsun Tribal Band sang and danced in traditional garb, burned a ceremonial fire, and prayed to heal the land and the people. Feelings of blessings and happiness filled those who had waited generations for this occasion.

"Our ceremony announced to our ancestors that we were back and we will make sure that they are never forgotten, ignored, or erased from history," said Amah Mutsun chairman, Valentin Lopez.

"It took my breath away," recalled Tribal elder Eleanor Castro. "This ceremony shows all that we are still here. The people will thrive and become a great nation again."

That connection is hard to top, but the Amah Mutsun are not the only ones who treasure the Bay Area's mountains. More than 7 million people live in their shadow, though they are shorter than those in the state's other areas, topped by Mount Saint Helena at 4,343 feet. Most stand within state and regional parks.

Tectonic plate movement, weathering, and erosion shaped these peaks. The San Andreas Fault and others make the region earthquake-prone. Major temblors occurred in 1989, and especially in 1906, when most San Francisco buildings fell or burned to the ground. Weaker quakes occur frequently, though most cause no property damage and often escape the notice of longtime residents.

The Bay Area's friendly climate makes these mountains accessible year-round, and their moderate size makes them ideal for beginning hikers. Some even allow driving to points near the summits, like Mount Umunhum.

Amah Mutsun, Muwekma, and other Ohlone descendants continue to hold ceremonies there, "because it is close to the Creator, because of its resonance to the spiritual self, and because it is where the children of their ancestors continue to reach out for balance and harmony."

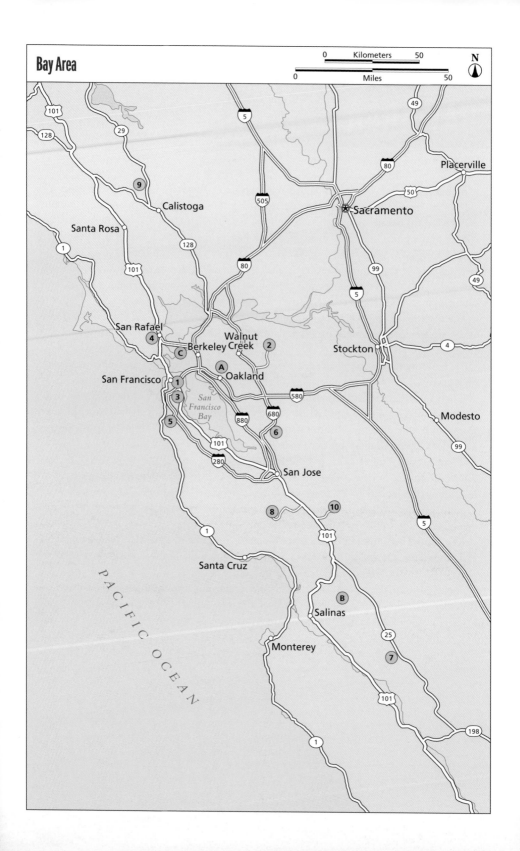

Bay Area

Bay Area Peaks at a Glance

SUMMIT	DISTANCE	DIFFICULTY	LAND AGENCY	SUMMIT ELEVATION	ELEVATION GAIN	BEST SEASON
1. Mount Davidson	0.5 mile	easy	Mount Davidson Park	928 feet	141 feet	year-round
2. Mount Diablo	1 mile	easy	Mount Diablo State Park	3,894 feet	129 feet	year-round
3. San Bruno Mountain	3.3 miles	easy to moderate	San Bruno Mountain State Park	1,314 feet	714 feet	year-round
4. Mount Tamalpais	4 miles	moderate	Mount Tamalpais State Park	2,571 feet	1,611 feet	year-round
5. Montara Mountain	6.4 miles	moderate	San Pedro Valley County Park	1,898 feet	1,714 feet	year-round
6. Mission Peak	7 miles	moderate	Mission Peak Regional Preserve	2,520 feet	1,980 feet	year-round
7. Hawkins Peak	5 miles	moderate	Pinnacles National Park	2,720 feet	1,450 feet	Aug–Dec
8. Mount Umunhum	7.4 miles	moderate	Sierra Azul Open Space Preserve	3,486 feet	1,166 feet	year-round
9. Mount Saint Helena	10 miles	moderate to strenuous	Robert Louis Stevenson State Park	4,343 feet	2,083 feet	spring and fall
10. Mount Sizer	14 miles	strenuous	Henry W. Coe State Park	3,216 feet	3,980 feet	spring and fall
A. Redwood Peak	1 mile	easy	Reinhardt Redwood Regional Park	1,619 feet	158 feet	year-round
B. Fremont Peak	1 mile	easy	Fremont Peak State Park	3,170 feet	350 feet	year-round
C. Mount Livermore	4 miles	easy	Angel Island State Park	781 feet	781 feet	year-round

Mount Davidson

1 MOUNT DAVIDSON

Shortest of this collection's summits in both height and distance, Mount Davidson still looks mountainous as San Francisco's highest perch, giving visitors an alpine feeling as they look over the city and Bay. A large concrete cross capping the mountain connects to an interesting history. Compared to the city's better-known Twin Peaks vista, Mount Davidson attracts little attention but deserves a visit.

Distance: 0.5 mile on a loop (all on trails)
Time: Less than 1 hour
Difficulty: Class 1; easy
Land agency: Mount Davidson Park
Nearest facilities: San Francisco

Trailhead elevation: 787 feet
Summit elevation: 928 feet
Elevation gain: 141 feet
Best season: Year-round
Permits: None needed

FINDING THE TRAILHEAD

Mount Davidson Park covers 40 acres straddling the Sherwood Forest and Miraloma neighborhoods near the city's geographic center. Our trailhead stands north of Dalewood Way near its intersections with Lansdale Avenue and Myra Way. Muni's 36 bus line provides a public transportation option.

CLIMBING THE MOUNTAIN

Our trail begins north of Dalewood Way just west of the bus stop. Climb through a thick, green forest. This hill was without trees as late as 1887 when then-owner Adolph Sutro planted a forest of eucalyptus. Now the trees are so dense that hikers feel removed from the surrounding city within just a few steps. After about 150 yards, make a sharp left at a trail junction. Then follow the path as it turns sharply right and leads to the summit area.

By now hikers will have seen the 103-foot-tall cross standing reverently to the west. There's quite a story here, and it's worth a few minutes of your time to see it more closely.

Our best view of the city lies to the east, where visitors can see the downtown high-rises and also native wildflowers, grasses, and shrubs on the mountain's northeastern slope.

To complete a counterclockwise loop, depart the summit area by hiking down a west-bound dirt road that curves to the south and ends at Dalewood Way, a few hundred feet west of our starting point and the bus stop.

MILES AND DIRECTIONS

0.0   From Dalewood Way, hike north on trail

0.1   At trail junction, turn left (west)

0.25 Summit; descend on westbound trail

0.5   Arrive back at the trailhead

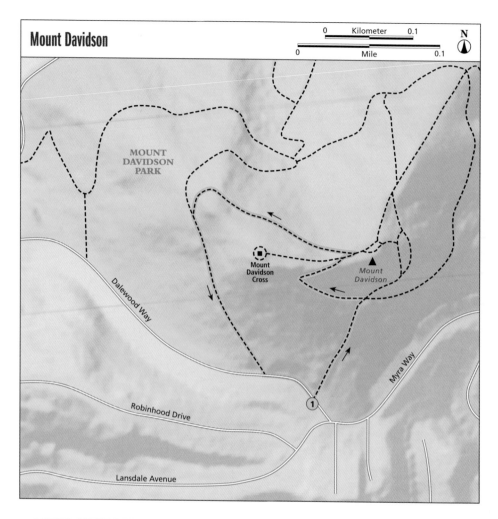

0   Kilometer   0.1

N

0   Mile   0.1

MOUNT
DAVIDSON
PARK

Mount
Davidson
Cross

Mount
Davidson

Dalewood Way

Myra Way

Robinhood Drive

1

Lansdale Avenue

HIGH HISTORY: CROSS CROWNS CITY'S CREST

Spanish captain Fernando Rivera climbed the mountain in heavy rain and wind during December 1774, the first recorded ascent, though surely not the first, as the indigenous Ramaytush had long inhabited the future city. Later, those inspired by its colorful wildflowers called it Blue Mountain.

This summit's contemporary name honors George Davidson (1825–1911), a surveyor and charter member of the Sierra Club. The mountaintop became a city park in 1929 thanks to Madie Brown and a committee she led, which bought 20 acres for public use, and Emma Baldwin, who donated 6 acres more.

Worshippers built the first wooden cross in 1923. Four other crosses followed over the next decade; fire destroyed three, and the fourth blew down. Undeterred, supporters raised $20,000 for the 103-foot concrete cross that still stands today, built with 750 cubic yards of concrete and 30 tons of reinforcing steel. President Franklin Roosevelt first lit the new cross by telegraph on March 24, 1934, and Easter sunrise services have followed ever since.

Mount Davidson and its historic cross occupy the highest ground in San Francisco.

The American Civil Liberties Union and other groups sued San Francisco over the cross in 1990, claiming its presence on public land violated the constitutional separation of church and state. The city lost the lawsuit and sold the cross and the 0.38 acre it stands upon to the Council of Armenian American Organizations of Northern California for $26,000 in 1997. The group dedicated the cross and a plaque at its base to the victims of the 1915 Armenian Genocide.

MORE MOUNTAIN MATTERS

Hikers can ascend Mount Davidson using five other trails starting at points surrounding the park on Dalewood Way, Juanita Way, Rockdale Drive, La Bica Way, and Molimo Drive.

Clint Eastwood filmed a scene for a 1971 movie at the cross, where "Dirty Harry" tries to catch a masked kidnapper—but no spoilers here!

A bolt ladder on the cross once allowed properly equipped climbers to reach its top, but the bolts were removed after the city sold the cross.

2 **MOUNT DIABLO**

A leisurely walk around and to the summit introduces hikers to the mountain's flora and its history. Few other peaks offer such an attainable experience on a summit that affords views of both the Pacific Ocean and the Sierra Nevada.

Distance: 1 mile on a loop (all on trails)
Time: 1 hour
Difficulty: Class 1; easy
Land agency: Mount Diablo State Park

Nearest facilities: Danville or Walnut Creek
Trailhead elevation: 3,720 feet
Summit elevation: 3,849 feet
Elevation gain: 129 feet
Best season: Year-round
Permits: None needed

FINDING THE TRAILHEAD

Enter Mount Diablo State Park from either Danville via South Gate Road or Walnut Creek via North Gate Road. The two roads meet at Junction Ranger Station where Summit Road begins. Take this to the lower summit parking area. The trail begins to the east.

CLIMBING THE MOUNTAIN

Mary Bowerman Trail begins north of the road and circles the summit in a clockwise direction. The name of the path honors a co-founder of Save Mount Diablo and botanist who studied the flora of the mountain for seventy years. The hike begins under oaks and passes deposits of greenstone, graywacke, chert, quartz, and shale. Soon we arrive at a viewing area complete with mounted telescopes. This portion of the trail is paved and accessible to wheelchairs.

As the trail circles to the summit's east side, trees give way to chaparral. To the east stands Devils Pulpit, a prominent formation of red chert. According to Miwok legend, the condor Mol'-luk perched there to watch over the world before the dawn of man. Our lap around the summit concludes along the sunnier south face through oats, foxtails, and junipers.

Now cross the road to join the eastbound Summit Trail. Yes, you could have skipped Mary Bowerman Trail and gone straight here, but the entire trip is only a mile long; live a little! Our path rejoins the swath of oaks before arriving at the top where the castle-like Summit Museum stands. Visible in clear conditions are Mount Tamalpais, the Golden Gate Bridge, and San Francisco to the west, and the Central Valley and Sierra Nevada to the east. Just a mile to the northeast, North Peak may entice viewers to take a longer outing. A short walk to the west returns us to the lower summit parking area.

MILES AND DIRECTIONS

0.0   From the lower summit parking area, hike east to start Mary Bowerman Trail

0.6   As Mary Bowerman Trail ends, cross the road to join Summit Trail

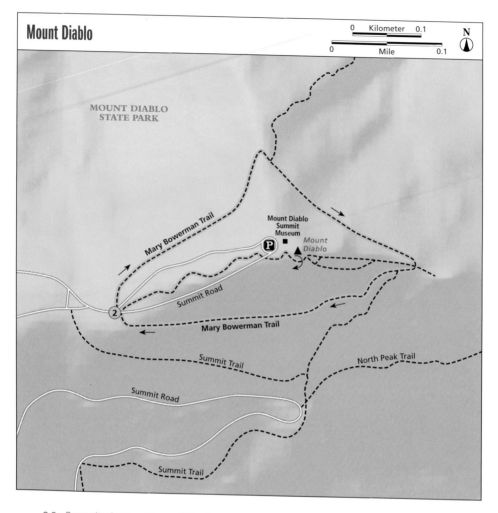

0.8 Summit; descend Summit Trail or the adjacent road to the lower parking area

1.0 Arrive back at the trailhead

HIGH HISTORY: SPANISH SKIRMISH SWAYS SOBRIQUET

Collision of tectonic plates pushed volcanic basalt, chert, and sandstone beneath the Pacific Ocean to the surface about 4 million years ago. Erosion over the next 2 million years shaped the rock into the largely sandstone mountain we recognize today.

Indigenous people inhabited the mountain and its surroundings for some 5,000 years. Ohlone called it *Tuyshtak*, meaning "at the dawn of time." Miwok named it *Oo'-yum-bel'-le*, and Nisenan called it *Sukkú Jaman*. Native Americans considered the mountain sacred and the center of creation.

The Spanish called it *Sierra de los Bolbones*, referencing the Bolbones people who lived at the foot of the mountain. The origin of the name "Mount Diablo" may stem from a skirmish between the Spanish and Chupcan who escaped from a mission in 1805. Angry that their foes defeated them and escaped, the Spanish called the spot near modern-day Concord *Monte del Diablo*, or "Devil's Woods." Apparently English-speaking settlers later applied the name to the mountain about 10 miles away.

With Senator William Sharkey as a key supporter, Mount Diablo State Park formed on 630 acres in 1921. The Civilian Conservation Corps labored on multiple roads and facilities projects between 1933 and 1942, including the castle-like Summit Museum. A beacon atop the building guided airplanes through nighttime skies until World War II; today it is lit each December 7 in memory of the 1941 Pearl Harbor attack.

Supporters such as Dr. Mary Bowerman and Art Bonwell founded Save Mount Diablo in 1971. Many environmentalists labored to preserve and expand the park, which now contains about 20,000 acres. More than forty parks and preserves on and around the mountain protect a total of 110,000 acres.

Neighboring North Peak provides another summit opportunity.

San Bruno Mountain

3 SAN BRUNO MOUNTAIN

An island of wilderness divides surrounding urban San Francisco and Peninsula communities. San Bruno Mountain provides welcome outdoor relief to millions of nearby city dwellers with its unique ecosystem, easily accessible trails, and rewarding summit view overlooking both the Pacific Ocean and the Bay.

Distance: 3.3 miles on a loop (all on trails)
Time: 2 to 3 hours
Difficulty: Class 1; easy to moderate
Land agency: San Bruno Mountain State and County Park

Nearest facilities: Daly City
Trailhead elevation: 714 feet
Summit elevation: 1,314 feet
Elevation gain: 600 feet
Best season: Year-round
Permits: None needed

FINDING THE TRAILHEAD

Take Guadalupe Canyon Parkway between Brisbane and Daly City and turn into San Bruno Mountain State and County Park, at the road's high point on its north side. After the entry station, turn right and go under the overpass to a parking area and trailhead south of the highway.

CLIMBING THE MOUNTAIN

Our trail leads southwest for about 150 yards. In response to the COVID-19 pandemic, park officials in 2020 designated Summit Loop Trail as one-way-only in a counterclockwise direction, so turn right at the first junction. Coastal scrub, coastal strand, oaks, and chaparral line our path; in all, the mountain supports more than 400 native plants, including 14 rare or endangered species.

Our path climbs gradually as it curves around the west side of the mountain, eventually taking us to Radio Road and transmission towers that began broadcasting radio and television signals in the 1950s. Before continuing our loop, you may want to walk a quarter-mile south on Radio Road to an inviting viewpoint beside a parking area. To gain the true summit, scramble up the rock to the west about halfway down the road.

Visitors can hope for an impressive view from this peak at the northern end of the Santa Cruz Mountains, including Mount Tamalpais to the north, Mount Diablo to the east, and Farallon Islands to the west. Visitors have earned that view, but they may not get it if fog surrounds the mountain, as it often does!

Resuming our route, Summit Loop Trail descends the mountain's north slope, making a few sharp turns as it drops several hundred feet. The trail weaves through rocky outcroppings; graywacke, a kind of sandstone, is the mountain's most common rock. Turn left at the next two junctions to return to our trailhead.

MILES AND DIRECTIONS

0.0 From the trailhead south of the highway, hike southwest

0.1 Turn right (northwest)

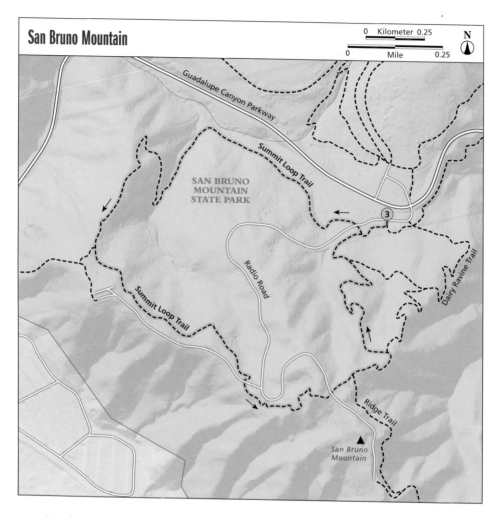

San Bruno Mountain

SAN BRUNO MOUNTAIN STATE PARK

Guadalupe Canyon Parkway

Summit Loop Trail

Radio Road

Summit Loop Trail

Dairy Ravine Trail

Ridge Trail

San Bruno Mountain

0 Kilometer 0.25

0 Mile 0.25

N

2.4 Cross Radio Road and continue loop trail to the east (or turn right/south for optional detour to vista at road's end)

2.4 Stay left (east)

2.6 Stay left (west)

3.0 Stay left (west)

3.2 Turn right (east)

3.3 Arrive back at the trailhead

HIGH HISTORY: BUTTERFLIES BEAT BULLDOZERS

Buckling of the Earth's crust caused the mountain's uplift from the ocean floor. Native Americans, including the Ohlone and Costanoan peoples, inhabited the mountain area for at least 5,000 years. Five Spanish soldiers made the first documented ascent of the mountain on December 2, 1774, and named it for a patron saint.

San Bruno Mountain looks down on Daly City and the Pacific Ocean.

As cities grew around the mountain in the twentieth century, epic battles ensued between developers and conservationists over the coveted land. Builders planned high-rise apartment buildings, office buildings, and golf courses; one plan would have leveled the mountain and deposited 200 million cubic yards of rock in the Bay for an airport. The Committee to Save San Bruno Mountain formed in 1973; activists such as David Schooley, Bette Higgins, and Fred Smith flooded public meetings in protest to demand "No New City on San Bruno Mountain!"

San Bruno Elfin and Mission Blue butterflies were listed as endangered species in 1976, which hindered development. By 1980, San Mateo County had raised money and acquired land to create a park, which has grown to 2,416 acres. Despite a groundbreaking habitat conservation plan, which supervisor Edward Bacciocco Jr. helped to negotiate, conflicts continued over the construction and protection of the endangered butterflies for many years. Nonetheless, San Bruno Mountain has since become one of the largest protected open spaces near an urban area in the United States.

MORE MOUNTAIN MATTERS

Fog peaks in the summer months, so for best viewing, choose a different season. Dress for cold wind, which gusts here frequently.

Though bicycles are not allowed on the Summit Loop Trail, other trails are open to them, and cyclists pedal up and down Radio Road frequently.

4 MOUNT TAMALPAIS

Dirt roads and trails lead up the slopes of an inviting coastal mountain to an inspiring summit overlooking San Francisco Bay. Our suggested route is one among hundreds of possible variations and introduces hikers to a Bay Area scenic gem.

Distance: 4 miles round-trip (on dirt roads and trails)
Time: 3 to 5 hours
Difficulty: Class 1; moderate
Land agency: Mount Tamalpais State Park

Nearest facilities: Mill Valley
Trailhead elevation: 960 feet
Summit elevation: 2,571 feet
Elevation gain: 1,611 feet
Best season: Year-round
Permits: None needed

FINDING THE TRAILHEAD

Take Highway 1 between Highway 101 and Muir Beach. Turn north onto Panoramic Highway and drive about 2.5 miles to the intersection with Edgewood Avenue. Park in a public lot west of the highway. Find Hogback Road north of Panoramic Highway and about 100 yards north from the parking lot.

CLIMBING THE MOUNTAIN

Our climb begins on Hogback Road, a dirt road leading past a fire station and northwest into the state park. On this journey visitors will see abundant chaparral, oaks, and redwoods. Wildflowers in season include lupine, Douglas iris, blue-eyed grass, and, of course, California poppies. The mountain boasts more than 750 species of plants in all.

Continue climbing north as the fire road intersects Matt Davis Trail and Hoo-Koo-E-Koo Trail. At 0.6 mile, we meet Old Railroad Grade Road. Turn left (northwest) to climb along the former path of the historic Mount Tamalpais Scenic Railway, "the crookedest railroad in the world."

About a mile from our start, Old Railroad Grade Road meets Fern Creek Trail. Heading west on Old Railroad Grade Road for about a mile would take you to the rustic and historic West Point Inn, a comfortable refuge surrounded by natural splendor. But for the shortest route to East Peak, turn right onto Fern Creek Trail, which leads to a visitor center and parking area beneath the summit. Yes, you could have driven here, but you'll enjoy the outing more this way!

Plank Walk Trail climbs the final steps to the rocky pinnacle, which boasts a Bay Area view like no other. Here visitors will also find Gardner Fire Lookout, a 1930s Civilian Conservation Corps project, which still sees summer use. Enjoy this beloved beauty before descending.

MILES AND DIRECTIONS

0.0 From the start of Hogback Road, hike north

0.6 Turn left (northwest) onto Old Railroad Grade Road

1.0 Turn right (north) onto Fern Creek Trail

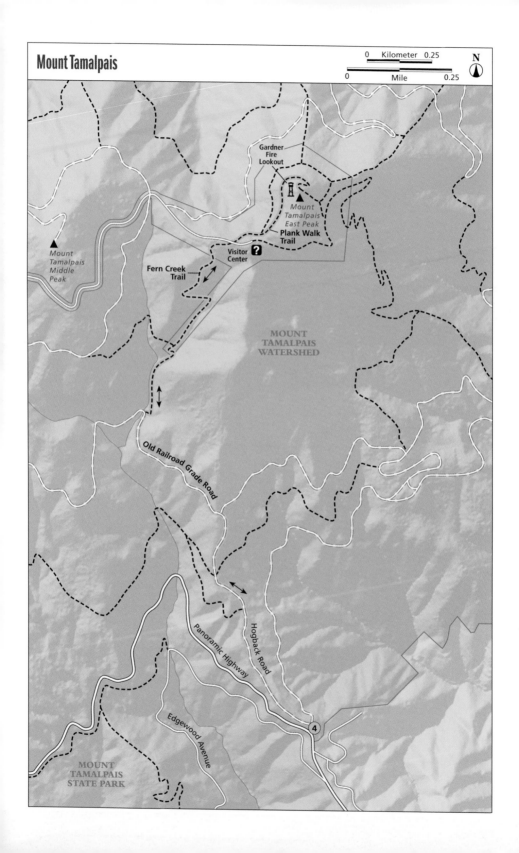

Mount Tamalpais

0   Kilometer   0.25

0   Mile   0.25

N

Gardner
Fire
Lookout

*Mount
Tamalpais
East Peak*

**Plank Walk
Trail**

*Mount
Tamalpais
Middle
Peak*

Visitor
Center

**Fern Creek
Trail**

MOUNT
TAMALPAIS
WATERSHED

Old Railroad Grade Road

Panoramic Highway

Hogback Road

4

Edgewood Avenue

MOUNT
TAMALPAIS
STATE PARK

Mount Tamalpais boasts a peerless view of San Francisco Bay.

1.7   Take Plank Walk Trail

2.0   Summit

4.0   Arrive back at the trailhead

HIGH HISTORY: "THE CROOKEDEST RAILROAD IN THE WORLD"

The collision of the Pacific and North America tectonic plates along the San Andreas Fault caused the uplift of the mountain, geologists believe. Millions of years of erosion exposed and shaped the rocky peaks and ridges visible today.

Coastal Miwok lived on and around the mountain for at least 3,000 years. Their word *tamalpais*, which means "coast mountain," outlasted several Spanish monikers to become the contemporary name.

MORE MOUNTAIN MATTERS

Mount Tamalpais marks the highest point of Marin County.

Bicycles are legal on paved roads and fire roads, but not hiking trails. Cyclists can access East Peak by starting our suggested route and staying on Old Railroad Grade Road until it meets East Ridgecrest Boulevard near the parking area.

Those wanting an easy hike can drive to East Peak parking area and hike 0.3 mile up Plank Walk Trail. Another family-friendly and worthwhile walk is Verna Dunshee Trail, which leads 0.6 mile around and beneath the summit.

Mount Tamalpais State Park charges no entry fee but does charge for parking in the East Peak parking area and a few others.

After the Gold Rush caused the population of San Francisco to explode, Mount Tamalpais became a popular recreational destination. Californians built a wagon road to the summit by 1884, and then a railroad by 1896. The Mount Tamalpais Scenic Railway negotiated 281 curves to deliver passengers to a mountaintop hotel, restaurant, and tavern, operating until 1930.

The Tamalpais Conservation Club organized to preserve the mountain in 1912. William and Elizabeth Kent donated 200 acres to help create a state park in 1928. Conservationists labored to dramatically increase the size of the park over time; it now contains 6,300 acres and completely encompasses Muir Woods National Monument.

5 MONTARA MOUNTAIN

A moderate climb leads through a lush forest onto a coastal peak with sweeping views of the ocean and Santa Cruz Mountains. Multiple trail options allow a variety of experiences and flora and fauna viewing opportunities.

Distance: 6.4 miles round-trip (on trails and dirt roads)	**Nearest facilities:** Pacifica
	Trailhead elevation: 184 feet
Time: 3 to 5 hours	**Summit elevation:** 1,898 feet
Difficulty: Class 1; moderate	**Elevation gain:** 1,714 feet
Land agency: San Pedro Valley County Park	**Best season:** Year-round
	Permits: None needed

FINDING THE TRAILHEAD

Enter San Pedro Valley County Park using Trout Farm Road in Pacifica. Our trail begins in the southwest corner of the parking area.

CLIMBING THE MOUNTAIN

Hike southwest on Montara Mountain Trail beneath a canopy of oak and eucalyptus trees. Our path ascends switchbacks on the mountain's north flank. As we climb, we can hope to see bobcats, black-tailed deer, rabbits, and the occasional gray fox. At 1.2 miles, pass a trail junction; go straight to continue ascending, but make a mental note of Brooks Creek Trail, which offers an alternative return route you could choose when descending.

Views improve as we climb above the trees into hillsides of chaparral, manzanita, and coastal scrub. Shortly after another set of switchbacks, turn left as the path intersects North Peak Access Road. By this point we have entered Montara State Beach. The dirt road winds its way southeast as it climbs toward our destination.

The San Francisco Public Utilities Commission owns the summit area, and some hikers were surprised to find it fenced off in 2019. The agency claimed it acted to protect habitat of the endangered San Bruno Elfin butterfly. Though at this writing hikers cannot legally access the mountain's very highest ground, they can come within a stone's throw of it and can still reach other points, like nearby Middle Peak (1,871 feet), about a quarter-mile west of North Peak. On clear days, the entire summit area boasts fine views

---

MORE MOUNTAIN MATTERS

Fog peaks here in summer. For best views, visit at other times.

An alternative route starts at Montara State Beach and follows North Peak Access Road. About 1.3 miles south of the Tom Lantos Tunnels, look east of Highway 1 for McNee Ranch Gate and a small parking area where the road begins. Look closely, because there's no sign and it can be hard to spot. Dogs and bicycles are legal on this 7-mile round-trip route, which avoids San Pedro Valley County Park and its entrance fee, though it's steeper and offers no shade.

Montara Mountain

Montara Mountain's summit offers visitors views of San Bruno Mountain, Mount Davidson, and Mount Tamalpais.

of the Santa Cruz Mountains, Pacific Ocean, and Farallon Islands. Look also for hawks and turkey vultures circling overhead.

For variety on the descent, consider turning right onto Brooks Creek Trail. This variation leads past Brooks Falls and San Pedro Creek (where steelhead trout spawn) at nearly the same distance to the parking area.

MILES AND DIRECTIONS

0.0   From the parking area, hike southwest on Montara Mountain Trail

1.2   At trail junction, go straight (southwest)

2.2   At road junction, go left (southeast) on North Peak Access Road

3.2   Summit

6.4   Arrive back at the trailhead

HIGH HISTORY: PRESERVATION PREVENTS RUINOUS ROAD

Geologists believe Montara once connected to a large mass of granite in the Southern Sierra. Plate tectonics broke apart this Salinian Block and moved the future mountain along the San Andreas Fault System about 200 miles to the north, while its other half remains near Bakersfield.

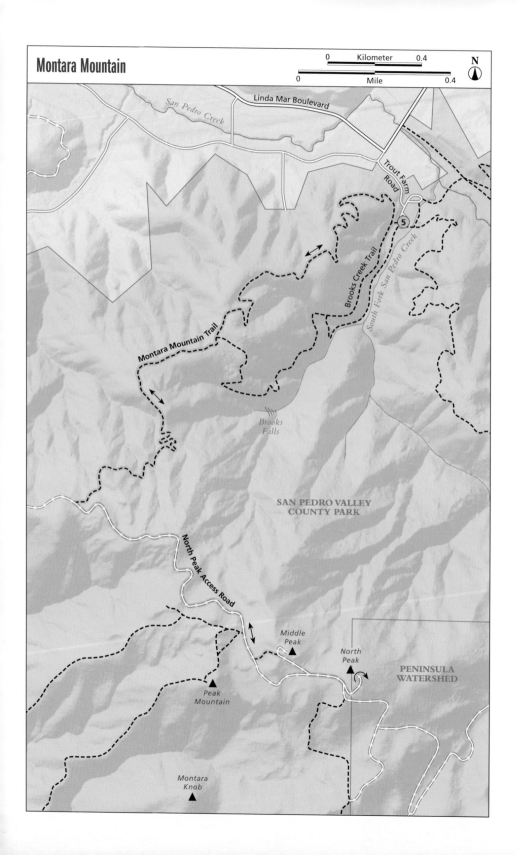

Montara Mountain

0 Kilometer 0.4
0 Mile 0.4

N

San Pedro Creek

Linda Mar Boulevard

Trout Farm Road

5

Brooks Creek Trail

South Fork San Pedro Creek

Montara Mountain Trail

Brooks Falls

SAN PEDRO VALLEY
COUNTY PARK

North Peak Access Road

Middle Peak ▲

North Peak ▲

PENINSULA WATERSHED

Peak Mountain ▲

Montara Knob ▲

The Aramai lived in Montara's shadow beside San Pedro Creek for some 9,000 years. Their villages were called Pruristac and Timigtac. The Spanish arrived in 1769 and established an outpost in San Pedro Valley, which would later become part of Pacifica.

The Whitney Survey labeled the mountain as "Moronto" in 1867, and the Coast Survey penned its current name in 1869; both names could be variations of the Spanish *montaña*, or *montaraz*.

Native Americans and Spanish and American settlers built trails and eventually dirt roads over the mountain range. After Highway 1 along the coast suffered repeated landslide damage, planners in 1958 began preparing to build a paved road over Montara Mountain but community and environmental opposition stalled the project. Decades of further landslides led to more road proposals and more resistance. Finally government officials decided to build twin tunnels that were completed in 2013 and named for Congressman Tom Lantos, a key supporter.

6 MISSION PEAK

A well-traveled trail just minutes from Silicon Valley takes hikers to a summit overlooking San Francisco Bay and surrounding East Bay plains and peaks. The "Mission Peeker" summit pole features tubes pointing to other Bay Area landmarks and ranks among the most popular photography sites in Alameda County.

Distance: 7 miles round-trip (on trails and dirt roads)
Time: 3 to 5 hours
Difficulty: Class 1; moderate
Land agency: Mission Peak Regional Preserve

Nearest facilities: Fremont
Trailhead elevation: 540 feet
Summit elevation: 2,520 feet
Elevation gain: 1,980 feet
Best season: Year-round
Permits: None needed

FINDING THE TRAILHEAD

 Park at or near Ohlone College on Mission Boulevard in Fremont. Parking is limited in this neighborhood, so paying a small sum to park in a college lot may be your best move. Locate the main trailhead on Pine Street beside a parking garage.

CLIMBING THE MOUNTAIN

Take plenty of water, especially in hot weather, because there is none available on the trail.

From Pine Street, hike up the path as it curves above Aquatic Way. Turn right onto Peak Trail, which overlaps Bay Area Ridge Trail for the next 3 miles. Bay views improve as the trail steadily gains elevation.

Soon our path curves northeast and climbs between hills. Stay right (east) upon reaching the saddle between them. Then the route parallels Mill Creek Road for about half a mile; trees here provide welcome shade on hot days. At a sharp turn to the west, climbing steepens through a cattle-grazing area and beautiful rolling hills come into view to the east.

Our summit comes into view as we pass an outhouse, which has a bicycle rack (no bikes are allowed on the last trail segment, so you may want to lock up your ride here). Turn left at the next two quick trail junctions to stay on Peak Trail. Expect to see more hikers from here on as the path from Stanford Avenue has joined ours. Turn right where Bay Area Ridge Trail and Peak Trail split for the summit push.

Our path gets steeper and rougher in the final segment, but soon you will be on the summit, admiring the "Mission Peeker" pole and a view that includes Mount Tamalpais, Mount Diablo, the Hamilton Range, Coyote Hills, and Sunol Regional Wilderness.

MILES AND DIRECTIONS

0.0 From Pine Street, hike east

0.25 At junction, turn right (southeast) to join Peak Trail

Mission Peak affords views of Sunol Regional Wilderness.

1.1	Stay right (east) at saddle
1.8	Stay right (west) at junction
2.5	Turn left (east)
2.6	Turn left (east)
2.8	Turn right (southeast)
3.5	Summit
7.0	Arrive back at the trailhead

HIGH HISTORY: POLE PROMOTES POPULARITY

This peak takes its name from nearby Mission San Jose, which Spaniards established in 1797, though the mountain attracted relatively few climbers for many years after that. "Perhaps the denizens of this valley are so accustomed to the sight of Mission Peak that they fail to appreciate the dignity and individuality which it gives to the landscape ... the mountain has a majesty of its own," wrote Winifred Bendel in 1904.

Things changed after park ranger and sculptor Leonard Page and companions installed the iconic "Mission Peeker" pole in 1990. The landmark's makers aimed to promote recycling, rainforest preservation, and environmental protection with elements of the monument. The pole eventually became the most popular tourist attraction in Fremont, attracting thousands of sightseers each week, though most don't seem to know its

Mission Peak

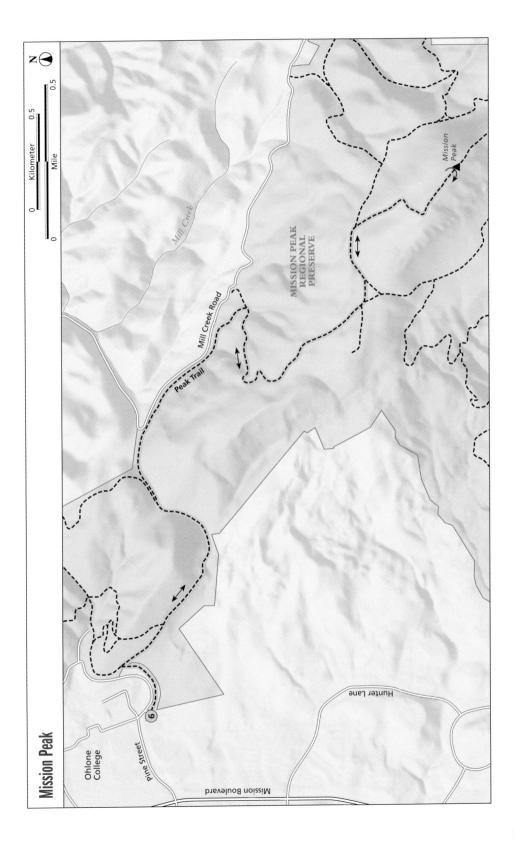

N

0   0.5   Kilometer   0.5

0   Mile

Ohlone College

Pine Street

Mission Boulevard

Hunter Lane

6

Peak Trail

Mill Creek Road

Mill Creek

MISSION PEAK
REGIONAL
PRESERVE

Mission
Peak

MORE MOUNTAIN MATTERS

Bikes are allowed on the preserve's dirt roads but not the summit path. The steep and bumpy terrain makes for difficult riding, though.

While dogs are legal, heat exhaustion kills some here every year. If you bring your furry friend, avoid hot days and carry more than enough water.

Though this guide suggests starting from Ohlone College, the most popular trailhead is Stanford Avenue Staging Area, which accesses a shorter but steeper climb. Parking is scarce and officers strictly enforce restrictions in the surrounding neighborhood. During weekends, you may have to park west of Mission Boulevard, adding a half-mile or more to your hike each way. Try this crowded route once and you'll see why the author suggests starting at Ohlone College!

intended environmental message. So much does the pole contribute to the mountain's popularity that local residents asked park officials to remove it to reduce parking congestion. Instead, officials have tried to appease the peak's neighbors by restricting parking and shortening park hours.

7 HAWKINS PEAK

Many people hike High Peaks Trail, but only a fraction of them visit Hawkins Peak, the highest point of Pinnacles' central mountain range. A loop hike with a short detour leads through the most spectacular and interesting section of the national park.

Distance: 5 miles on a loop (on trails and use trails)
Time: 3 to 4 hours
Difficulty: Class 1 (to the peak's base); moderate
Land agency: Pinnacles National Park

Nearest facilities: Pinnacles Campground
Trailhead elevation: 1,270 feet
Summit elevation: 2,720 feet
Elevation gain: 1,450 feet
Best season: Aug–Dec
Permits: None needed

FINDING THE TRAILHEAD

Take Highways 25 and 146 to enter the park's eastern entrance and park at Bear Gulch day-use area. Condor Gulch Trail leads to the northwest.

CLIMBING THE MOUNTAIN

Before you go, consider timing and access. The Hawkins Peak area closes each year for peregrine falcon nesting starting in January on the Tuesday after Martin Luther King Jr. Day and normally reopens by late July. The High Peaks Trail is usually open year-round but portions could close if necessary to protect falcons or condors. Check ahead on the park's website and consult trail signs for information.

Our adventure begins with a climb up the aptly named Condor Gulch Trail. Keep an eye out for condors and other raptors; spotting one could make your outing unforgettable. The trail zigs and zags as it climbs about 1,000 feet to High Peaks Trail. Turn left toward Hawkins Peak and hike about a half-mile.

Shortly after several sharp turns, look for a climbers' trail on the left or southeast of High Peaks Trail. This leads to the base of Hawkins Peak. Summiting the steep peak requires Class 5 climbing technique, but more easily achieved points a short distance to the south stand nearly as tall. We are now surrounded by unique rocky scenery, especially to the south. In that direction our trail continues through more high peaks, and North Chalone Peak—the park's highest point, capped by a fire lookout tower—stands about 3 miles away.

After returning to High Peaks Trail, turn left to continue following it to the south. Now the trail leads beside and over other steep formations of the range. In some places, the route ascends or descends grades that would normally send climbers after their ropes and gear. But thanks to the Great Depression–era Civilian Conservation Corps, stone-carved steps and steel rails take us through the steepest terrain.

High Peaks Trail continues its counterclockwise arc as it descends all the way to Bear Gulch day-use area, our start and finish point. Once you reach it, you will have completed the most rewarding trek in the park, hiked one of the most unique paths in California, and visited a rewarding little-known mountain.

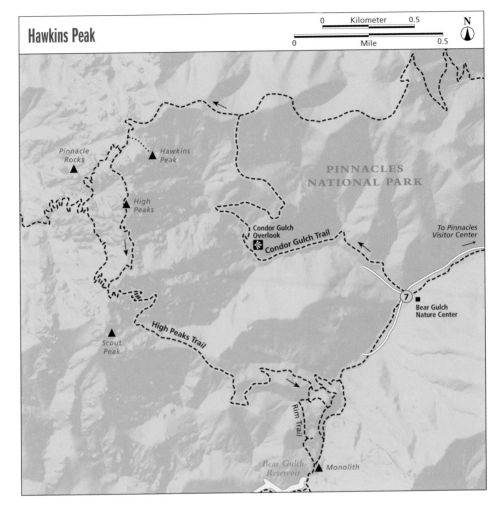

MILES AND DIRECTIONS

0.0 From Bear Gulch Nature Center, hike northwest on Condor Gulch Trail

1.0 Condor Gulch Overlook

1.6 Turn left (west) at High Peaks Trail junction

2.1 Turn left (southwest) onto climbers' trail

2.2 Reach the base of Hawkins Peak

2.3 Return to High Peaks Trail and turn left (south)

2.4 Stay left (southwest) to stay on High Peaks Trail

2.9 Turn left (southeast) to stay on High Peaks Trail

4.3 Turn left (southwest) at Rim Trail junction to stay on High Peaks Trail

4.4 Turn left (north) at junction to stay on High Peaks Trail

4.5 Go straight (north) at junction to stay on High Peaks Trail

The High Peaks Trail leads through the park's most spectacular scenery.

4.7   Cross road to stay on High Peaks Trail

5.0   Arrive back at the trailhead

HIGH HISTORY: MOBILE MINERALS, PRESIDENTIAL PROTECTION

Multiple volcanic eruptions some 23 million years ago followed by erosion formed these rocky peaks of andesite. Plate movement transported these pinnacles 195 miles northwest along the San Andreas Fault from their original location.

MORE MOUNTAIN MATTERS

Most visitors enter Pinnacles from the east, but be advised that the park's eastern parking lots fill up quickly on weekends, requiring visitors to take a shuttle.

A different hike leads to Hawkins Peak from the west. From Soledad, take Highway 146 to the park's Chaparral Trailhead Parking Area. Take Juniper Canyon Trail until it meets High Peaks Trail. Turn left to approach Hawkins Peak from the south. This 6-mile, out-and-back variation climbs about 1,300 feet.

To reach the actual summit of Hawkins Peak (which rock climbers call Tuff Dome) requires a climb of 5.6 difficulty.

Native American groups including the Mutsun and Chalon Tribes inhabited the area for at least 2,000 years. The Spanish built a mission in nearby Soledad in 1791. Homesteader Schuyler Hain, who became known as the "Father of the Pinnacles," arrived in 1891, led tours, and wrote articles urging preservation for twenty years.

President Teddy Roosevelt protected 2,000 acres as a national monument in 1908; the protected area would grow over time. Irv Hawkins served as the monument's custodian from 1925 to 1945, inspiring our mountain's name.

Rock climbers arrived in the 1930s and four Sierra Club members made the first recorded ascent of Hawkins Peak (including its technical summit, Tuff Dome) in 1933. Members of the Civilian Conservation Corps labored on improvements from 1933 through 1942. Congress designated 26,000 acres as a national park in 2013.

Mount Umunhum

8 MOUNT UMUNHUM

A well-groomed trail climbs through a forest to the site of a Cold War–era US Air Force base. Mount Um, as the locals call it, stands among the highest peaks of the Santa Cruz Mountains. Closed to the public for decades, it reopened to visitors in 2017.

Distance: 7.4 miles round-trip (all on trails)
Time: 3 to 5 hours
Difficulty: Class 1; moderate
Land agency: Sierra Azul Open Space Preserve

Nearest facilities: San Jose
Trailhead elevation: 2,320 feet
Summit elevation: 3,486 feet
Elevation gain: 1,166 feet
Best season: Year-round
Permits: None needed

FINDING THE TRAILHEAD

 Exit Highway 85 in San Jose at Camden Avenue and drive south for 1.8 miles. Turn right on Hicks Road and drive for 6.3 miles. Then turn right on Mount Umunhum Road and drive for 1.7 miles to reach Bald Mountain Parking Area.

CLIMBING THE MOUNTAIN

From Bald Mountain Parking Area, cross the road to find Mount Umunhum Trail leading west. Our path climbs gradually through a forest of pines and manzanita, providing shelter from wind and ample shade to cool a hot day. Take the short detour to enjoy Guadalupe Creek Overlook.

On its second half our path continues its westward push and climbs switchbacks, crossing Guadalupe Creek twice. Keep an eye out for a variety of wildlife, with more than 60 species of mammals including rabbits, foxes, and bobcats. Among more than 100 types of birds are eagles, hawks, owls, ravens, hummingbirds, and purple martins, the largest swallows in North America.

Near the trail's end, a spur path leads to a parking area. Astute hikers will observe that they could have driven to a lot near the summit, but take pride that you hiked it instead, and trek the final quarter-mile. From the east summit by the radar tower, we can see the ocean and the Bay Area's highest peaks in the distance: Mount Tamalpais, Mount Diablo, and Mount Hamilton.

MILES AND DIRECTIONS

0.0 From Bald Mountain Parking Area, cross the road and hike west on Mount Umunhum Trail

0.3 At Barlow Road junction, go straight to stay on-trail

1.3 Guadalupe Creek Overlook

3.5 Go straight at trail junction

3.7 Summit

7.4 Arrive back at the trailhead

Mount Umunhum

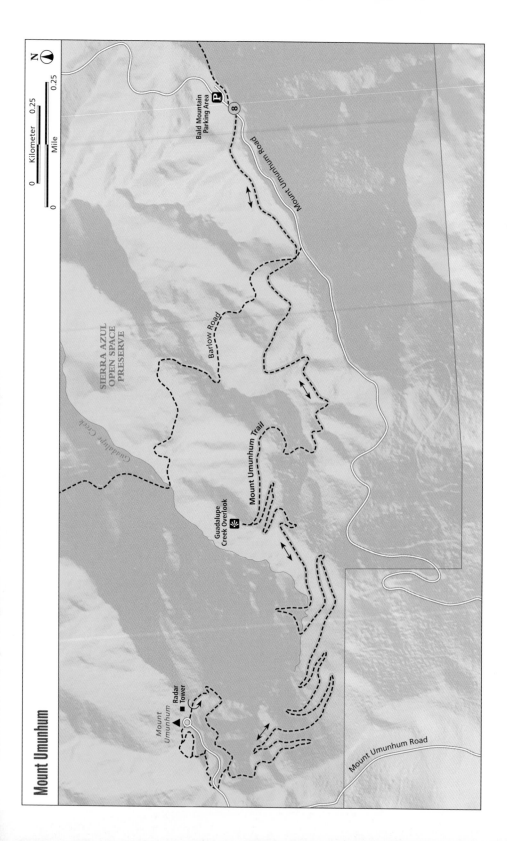

HIGH HISTORY: HUMMINGBIRD'S HEROISM AND "HEALING"

Ohlone people believe Mount Umunhum played a key role in the beginning of life. According to a creation story, Hummingbird used his bravery, quickness, and intelligence to retrieve fire from Badger people who did not want to share it. Hummingbird then brought fire to the top of Mount Umunhum where it ignited in Hummingbird's throat and turned it red.

The New Almaden Quicksilver mining operation was launched near here in 1845, unearthing the mountain's mercury, which was used to process gold during California's Gold Rush. After statehood in 1850, this became California's first legal mining claim.

Austrian and German refugees of the Franco-Prussian War settled on Umunhum's southwest slopes in the 1870s, building a community that remained for sixty years.

During the Cold War, the US government built Almaden Air Force Station, which guarded against Soviet nuclear bombers starting in 1957. Up to 125 personnel and their families lived and worked on the mountain for twenty-three years. Advancements in satellite technology led to the base's closure in 1980. However, many of the service members who worked here remained in the area to work in Silicon Valley. The 84-foot concrete tower that supported an enormous rotating radar dish still stands, making the mountain identifiable from miles around.

A Cold War–era radar building and a Native American ceremony area stand on Mount Umunhum's summit.

> **MORE MOUNTAIN MATTERS**
> Bring your own water, as there's none available at the summit area.
>   Cyclists can use both Mount Umunhum Road and Mount Umunhum Trail (except for the last quarter-mile, though a connector trail allows them to access the road here).
>   If 3.7 miles sounds better than 7.4 miles, hikers can complete a one-way trip if a driver meets them at the other end.

Midpeninsula Regional Open Space District purchased the 36-acre summit area in 1986 for $261,566. With the help of $3.2 million in federal funding and voter-approved bonds, the agency dismantled eighty Air Force buildings, removed 14,000 tons of waste, and opened the mountain to public access.

Red-throated hummingbirds still inhabit the mountain that the Ohlone named *Umunhum* in their honor. Native Americans still pray on the mountain for "past generations and future descendants, for healing, and for renewal of the environment."

9 MOUNT SAINT HELENA

A climb up the Bay Area's highest mountain combines abundant and interesting history, geology, and scenery. Those who ascend Mount Saint Helena deserve a little wine country indulgence more than most visitors to the vineyards below.

Distance: 10 miles round-trip (on trails and dirt roads)
Time: 4 to 6 hours
Difficulty: Class 1; moderate to strenuous
Land agency: Robert Louis Stevenson State Park

Nearest facilities: Calistoga
Trailhead elevation: 2,260 feet
Summit elevation: 4,343 feet
Elevation gain: 2,083 feet
Best seasons: Spring and fall
Permits: None needed

FINDING THE TRAILHEAD

Take Highway 29 between Calistoga and Middletown. There is limited parking on both sides of the road where it passes through Robert Louis Stevenson State Park. Stevenson Memorial Trail begins west of the highway.

CLIMBING THE MOUNTAIN

Hike west past a picnic area onto Stevenson Memorial Trail. Douglas fir, oak, and madrone trees shade the most rugged part of the outing as the rocky path climbs switchbacks. Our trail passes the Silverado mining area where a monument honors author Robert Louis Stevenson, who honeymooned with his wife here in 1880.

Turn left when the trail joins Mount Saint Helena Trail, which looks more like a dirt road. We'll take this the rest of the way as it climbs steadily northwest. Soon after the junction, you will pass a popular rock-climbing area called The Bubble as our path turns sharply east.

After the climbing eases around 3.4 miles, there are three optional turnoffs to reach sub-peaks, each involving short detours southwest of our main route. The third of these arrives at 4.4 miles from the trailhead and leads to the highest point in Napa County.

Our path crosses briefly into Lake County and then into Sonoma County to reach our main objective, North Peak. Here we find broadcast buildings and towers and replicas of the engraved plate Russians left in 1841. In addition, the summit view includes the park's 5,272 acres, Napa Valley, Mount Tamalpais, Mount Diablo, and even the distant Sierra Nevada.

MILES AND DIRECTIONS

0.0 From the parking area, hike Stevenson Memorial Trail

0.6 Stevenson Memorial

0.8 At trail junction, go left (south) to join Mount Saint Helena Trail

3.4 Go straight (northwest)

4.4 Go left (west)

5.0 Summit

10.0 Arrive back at the trailhead

Mount Saint Helena

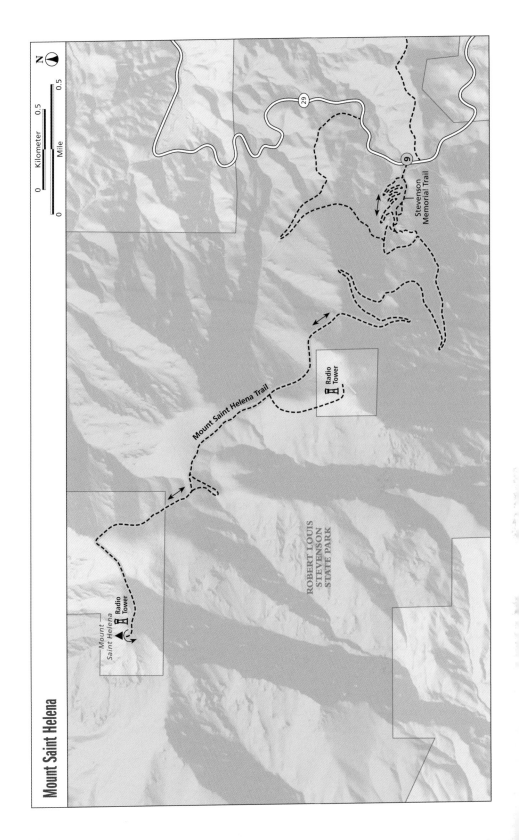

Mount Saint Helena

N

0   0.5   Kilometer   0.5

0   Mile   0.5

29

9

Stevenson Memorial Trail

Mount Saint Helena Trail

Radio Tower

Mount Saint Helena

Radio Tower

ROBERT LOUIS STEVENSON STATE PARK

Mount Saint Helena overlooks Napa, Lake, and Sonoma Counties.

HIGH HISTORY: A SAINT AND A SQUATTER

Volcanic eruptions beginning 3 million years ago gave rise to Mount Saint Helena and the neighboring Palisades. The Wappo called the mountain *Kanamota*. Spanish documents refer to it as *Serro de los Mallacomes*, in reference to another Native American tribe in the area.

At least three theories purport to explain the current name. First, the mountain reminded a Spanish friar of a carving he had once seen depicting Saint Helena in 1823. Second, a sea captain named it after his boat in 1844. And third, a Russian survey party climbed the mountain in 1841, naming it for Princess Helena de Gagarin, who was named after Saint Helena. A copper plate left on the summit documented the Russians' ascent, if not specifically the possibility that they so named the mountain.

Robert Louis Stevenson and Frances Osbourne Stevenson honeymooned in an abandoned mining camp on the mountain in 1880. In his book *The Silverado Squatters*, Stevenson described his ascent of the mountain. "The woods sang aloud, and gave largely of their healthful breath. Gladness seemed to inhabit these upper zones," he wrote. "There are days in a life when thus to climb out of the lowlands, seems like scaling heaven."

MORE MOUNTAIN MATTERS

This park and trailhead have become popular, so arrive early to find parking on weekends.

This route is accessible year-round, but heat makes the hike unpleasant in summer. Winter is feasible in the right conditions, but check the forecast, because the mountain sees cold winds and occasionally snow.

Cyclists cannot use Stevenson Memorial Trail but they can take Mount Saint Helena Trail the entire way to the summit. It begins on the west side of Highway 29, about a quarter-mile north of the main parking area.

10 **MOUNT SIZER**

Our toughest Bay Area mountain delves into an unspoiled and largely unknown wilderness within the Diablo Range on a route known as the Blue Ridge Loop. This makes a good trial run for higher mountains elsewhere in the state and works as a long day trip or an overnight journey.

Distance: 14 miles on a loop (on trails and dirt roads)
Time: 6 to 8 hours
Difficulty: Class 1; strenuous (for distance and elevation gain)
Land agency: Henry W. Coe State Park
Nearest facilities: Morgan Hill

Trailhead elevation: 2,672 feet
Summit elevation: 3,216 feet
Elevation gain: 3,980 feet (yes, that's right!)
Best seasons: Spring and fall
Permits: None needed for day use, required for overnight travel

FINDING THE TRAILHEAD

From Morgan Hill, take East Dunne Avenue 13 steep and winding miles to Coe Headquarters Park Entrance. Just past the entrance, Monument Trail leads north.

CLIMBING THE MOUNTAIN

Our route makes a clockwise loop involving big elevation gains and drops throughout. This hike dwarfs other Bay Area treks, but provides the ambitious with a first-rate workout and wilderness experience.

Monument Trail leads north from the park headquarters. A few switchbacks in the early going will warm up your muscles as the path passes oaks and pines. The trail joins northbound Hobbs Road in a half-mile, and our route stays atop a ridge before descending and crossing Little Coyote Creek. Then we reach Frog Lake; stop a moment to see and hear the amphibians that gave this pond its name.

Follow Frog Lake Trail as it climbs Middle Ridge, turns left onto Middle Ridge Trail, and pivots right to rejoin Hobbs Road. Here comes the first big drop as we descend 1,200 feet in a mile and a half to the canyon's bottom.

Take a break at Coyote Creek. Good news: You don't have to climb back up the hill you descended. But an even steeper climb awaits across the water. Take a drink before beginning The Shortcut, which gains 1,400 feet over the next 1.2 miles at an average 22 percent grade. This is the hardest portion of the hike, so take your time.

A bench atop Blue Ridge greets hardy hikers who overcome The Shortcut, and the author suggests you use it. Then turn right onto Blue Ridge Road as we begin the most scenic and enjoyable part of the hike. Wildflowers blanket these hills with color in spring.

Our path rolls gently for about a mile to the highest point of Blue Ridge, Mount Sizer. While the summit itself is unimpressive, it affords a rarely seen perspective of the Diablo Range to the east. You may spot golden eagles, turkey vultures, or other raptors flying above.

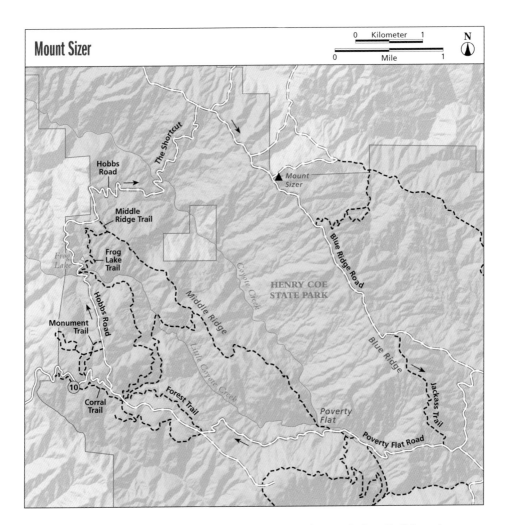

Continue southeast along Blue Ridge Road. Turn right onto Jackass Trail for a shorter and more interesting segment to the canyon bottom. Turn right onto Poverty Flat Road, which leads past three campsites and across Coyote Creek.

Our last push climbs another 1,400 feet but thankfully more gradually than earlier segments. Look north to see Blue Ridge, which you traversed earlier. For an up-close look at a variety of trees, take Forest Trail, which parallels Manzanita Point Road. Corral Trail returns to the park headquarters, completing the loop.

MILES AND DIRECTIONS

0.0 Hike north on Monument Trail

0.5 Stay left (north) as trail meets Hobbs Road

1.5 At Frog Lake, go north on Frog Lake Trail

2.2 At junction, turn left (northwest) onto Middle Ridge Trail

Trails through the park's wilderness feel far away from nearby Bay Area cities.

2.3 Turn right (northwest) onto Hobbs Road

3.9 Cross Coyote Creek and begin The Shortcut

5.1 Turn right (southeast) onto Blue Ridge Road

6.2 Summit

8.2 Turn right (southeast) onto Jackass Trail

9.5 Turn right (west) onto Poverty Flat Road

10.7 Traverse Coyote Creek

12.3 Turn right (west) onto Forest Trail

13.4 Turn right (west) onto Corral Trail

14.0 Arrive back at the trailhead

HIGH HISTORY: OUTLANDISH OUTLAWS, GENEROUS GRANT

Ohlone and Northern Valley Yokuts populated this area prior to the Spanish arrival in 1769. Some Native Americans later found work on cattle ranches near today's park.

Mexican sheepherders sheltered in adobe huts as they watched their flocks in the 1800s. Outlaws such as Joaquin Murrieta—a reputed horse thief sometimes called "The Robin Hood of the West"—hid in the hills. The Gold Rush brought miners who dug for quicksilver and copper. Ranchers grazed cattle from the 1880s into the 1960s, creating trails and roads still in use today.

Starting in 1858, New Hampshire native Henry Coe and sons Henry Jr. and Charles bought thousands of acres in the Diablo Range. After Henry Jr. died in 1943, his daughter Sada Sutcliffe Coe Robinson donated the land for a park. "May these quiet hills bring peace to the souls of those who are seeking," she expressed. Henry W. Coe State Park formed in 1958 and since then has grown to 87,000 acres.

Mount Sizer's name honors Samuel Sizer (1850–1885), a rancher from New York who bought 30 acres on Blue Ridge in 1883. He became friends with the Coes, though he died at age 35 of pneumonia.

MORE MOUNTAINS IN THE BAY AREA

A. REDWOOD PEAK

Distance: 1 mile round-trip (on trails)
Time: 1 hour
Difficulty: Class 1; easy
Land agency: Reinhardt Redwood Regional Park
Nearest facilities: Oakland
Trailhead elevation: 1,461 feet
Summit elevation: 1,619 feet
Elevation gain: 158 feet
Best season: Year-round
Permits: None needed

Redwood Peak

The East Bay Regional Park District renamed this park in 2019 after Dr. Aurelia Reinhardt, who helped to create the park district in 1934. Reinhardt became the first woman to serve on its board, and she led nearby Mills College as its president for twenty-seven years. Enter the park from Skyline Boulevard at Redwood Bowl and hike east and then north, following trail signs. Redwood trees obscure a summit view but provide a soothing ambience.

B. FREMONT PEAK

Distance: 1 mile on a loop (on trails and a dirt road)
Time: 1 hour
Difficulty: Class 1; easy
Land agency: Fremont Peak State Park
Nearest facilities: Hollister
Trailhead elevation: 2,820 feet
Summit elevation: 3,170 feet
Elevation gain: 350 feet
Best season: Year-round
Permits: None needed

Fremont Peak

After Mexican authorities ordered US troops out of California in 1846, army captain John Fremont and sixty men built camp near here and raised an American flag on a summit in defiance. The Mexican–American War began a month later. Start the loop trail from the upper parking area. The peak overlooks Monterey Bay, the San Benito Valley, and the Santa Lucia Mountains.

C. MOUNT LIVERMORE

Distance: 4 miles round-trip (on trails)
Time: 2 to 3 hours
Difficulty: Class 1; easy
Land agency: Angel Island State Park
Nearest facilities: Tiburon
Trailhead elevation: Sea level
Summit elevation: 781 feet
Elevation gain: 781 feet
Best season: Year-round
Permits: None needed

Mount Livermore

This island houses an immigration station where Chinese immigrants were detained and questioned from 1910 to 1940. The mountain's name honors Caroline Livermore, a Bay Area conservationist who helped protect Angel Island, Mount Tamalpais, and other areas. Most people take a ferry from San Francisco or Tiburon to reach the island. North Ridge Trail leads from Ayala Cove Ferry Terminal to the summit, which boasts a Bay Area view like no other.

Pismo Beach

Joshua Tree National Park

SOCAL

People who climbed Mount San Antonio (known to its friends as Mount Baldy) from 2007 to 2017 ran a good chance of meeting Seuk "Sam" Kim.

After retiring, the Korean American immigrant climbed the peak weekly or even daily in his 70s, once summiting the 10,064-foot mountain he loved more than 100 days in a row. Kim often took pictures and shared food with other hikers, rescuing more than a few who were in distress.

"Better than church, better than medicine," Kim once said of his mountain, and Mount Baldy's legions of admirers would agree.

SoCal (Southern California) possesses 24 million people, the majority of the state's population, as well as hundreds of miles of coastline and thousands of square miles of desert. Among thousands of mountains, 22 exceed 10,000 feet. Tectonic plate movement, volcanic activity, glaciation, and erosion all contributed to their formations.

A series of east–west Transverse Ranges, including the Santa Monica, San Gabriel, and San Bernardino Mountains, stand between SoCal and the more-northern part of California. The Mojave Desert fills much of the region's eastern side.

Many popular hikes, as well as most of this book's SoCal outings, stand within Angeles, Cleveland, Los Padres, and San Bernardino National Forests. Parking at their popular trailheads requires an Adventure Pass, available from the Forest Service or local retailers.

Summer brings hot temperatures, especially in the desert, making fall and spring preferable for outings in places like Joshua Tree National Park. Snow covers the region's taller mountains and closes high-country forest roads each winter, though shorter mountains near the coast are accessible year-round. A few snowy peaks are accessible in winter and early spring, like Mount Baldy.

Kim set a goal to climb that peak 1,000 times, completing some 800 ascents by age 79. He often climbed in rain, wind, and snow. But after Kim failed to return following a storm on April 7, 2017, a search team found him off-route and deceased.

The next month, more than 200 hikers summited Baldy in Kim's honor to symbolically help him meet his goal. Among them was David Kim, Sam's son. Kim's gravestone reads "The Spirit of Mt. Baldy."

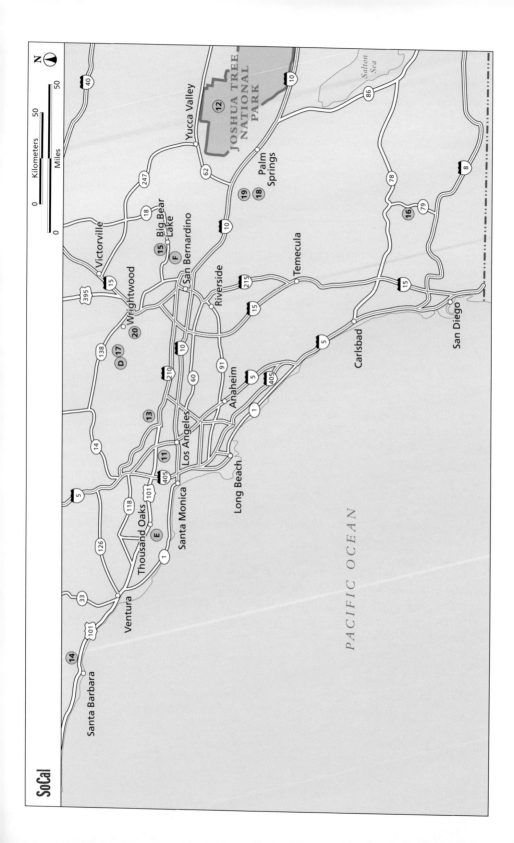

SoCal Peaks at a Glance

SUMMIT	DISTANCE	DIFFICULTY	LAND AGENCY	SUMMIT ELEVATION	ELEVATION GAIN	BEST SEASON
11. Mount Hollywood	2 miles	Class 1; easy	Griffith Park	1,625 feet	870 feet	year-round
12. Ryan Mountain	3 miles	Class 1; easy to moderate	Joshua Tree National Park	5,457	1,057 feet	Oct–May
13. Echo Mountain	5.4 miles	Class 1; moderate	Angeles National Forest	3,207	1,319 feet	year-round
14. Montecito Peak	6 miles	Class 2; moderate	Los Padres National Forest	3,214 feet	2,464 feet	year-round
15. Butler Peak	10 miles	Class 1, moderate	San Bernardino National Forest	8,535 feet	1,426 feet	May–Nov
16. Cuyamaca Peak	7.7 miles	Class 1, moderate	Cuyamaca Rancho State Park	6,512 feet	1,834 feet	year-round
17. Mount Baden-Powell	8.2 miles	Class 1, moderate	Angeles National Forest	9,407 feet	2,792 feet	May–Nov
18. Tahquitz Peak	8.2 miles	Class 1, moderate	San Bernardino National Forest	8,846 feet	2,346 feet	May–Oct
19. San Jacinto Peak	10 miles	Class 2; moderate to strenuous	Mount San Jacinto State Park	10,804 feet	2,288 feet	May–Oct
20. Mount San Antonio	10 miles	Class 2; strenuous	Angeles National Forest	10,064 feet	3,905 feet	Apr–Nov
D. Throop Peak	3 miles	Class 1; easy	Angeles National Forest	9,138 feet	1,237 feet	May–Nov
E. Sandstone Peak	3 miles	Class 2; moderate	Santa Monica Mountains National Recreation Area	3,111 feet	1,050 feet	year-round
F. Keller Peak	12.2 miles	Class 1; moderate	San Bernardino National Forest	7,882 feet	1,855 feet	May–Nov

Mount Hollywood

11 MOUNT HOLLYWOOD

Our SoCal outings begin with an easy hike through the largest park in Los Angeles. Discover seven square miles of open space just a stone's throw from the world's moviemaking capital. As an added bonus, our mountain overlooks the famous Hollywood sign.

Distance: 2 miles round-trip (all on trails)
Time: 1 to 2 hours
Difficulty: Class 1; easy
Land agency: Griffith Park
Nearest facilities: Los Angeles

Trailhead elevation: 870 feet
Summit elevation: 1,625 feet
Elevation gain: 755 feet
Best season: Year-round
Permits: None needed

FINDING THE TRAILHEAD

To enter Griffith Park from the south, take Los Feliz Boulevard and turn north on North Vermont Canyon Road. Find public parking beside the picnic area and just north of the Greek Theater. Our trail begins east of the road and leads north.

CLIMBING THE MOUNTAIN

Hike north past the park's bird sanctuary, where you may view more than 200 species of feathered friends. Our path climbs and turns west to a five-way intersection. Take a sharp right for the shortest path to our destination.

After a short distance, we reach another intersection. Turning left or right on Charlie Turner Trail will take you past some popular photo opportunities on a slightly longer route to the peak. A western detour leads past picturesque palm trees. For the shortest approach, go straight.

Our summit features a picnic area, gymnastics bars, and a wide view of greater Los Angeles and the mountains that surround it, including San Gabriel Wilderness to the northeast. The Hollywood sign stands to the west. The shortest way back retraces our ascent route, but for a better look at the sign, consider detouring west toward the paved Mount Hollywood Drive.

MILES AND DIRECTIONS

0.0   From the parking area beside the Greek Theater, hike north

0.7   At five-way intersection, turn sharply right (north)

1.0   Summit

2.0   Arrive back at the trailhead

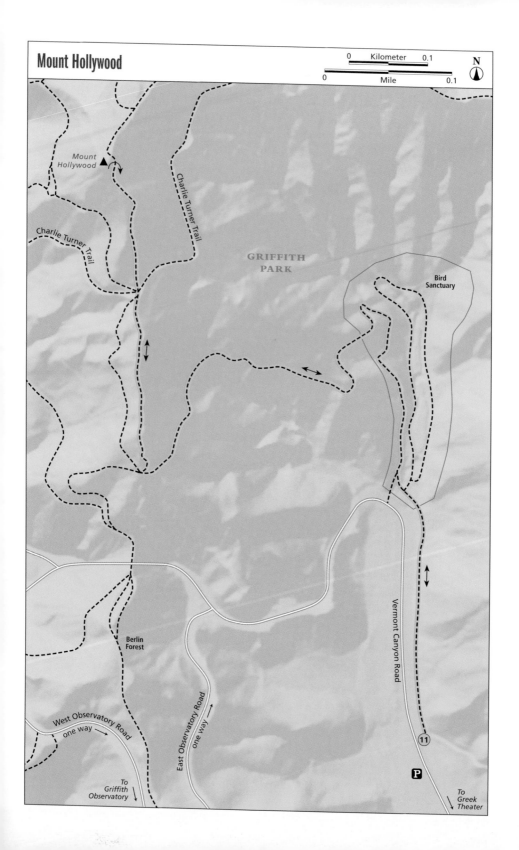

Mount Hollywood

Kilometer 0   0.1

Mile 0   0.1

N

Mount Hollywood ▲

Charlie Turner Trail

Charlie Turner Trail

GRIFFITH PARK

Bird Sanctuary

Berlin Forest

West Observatory Road
one way

East Observatory Road
one way

Vermont Canyon Road

11

P

To Griffith Observatory

To Greek Theater

Hikers earn a good view of the Hollywood sign by making an optional detour.

HIGH HISTORY: SPANISH SETTLERS, GENEROUS GIFT, SAVAGE SHOOTING

The Tongva Tribe inhabited this area long before any others. Spanish corporal Jose Feliz acquired a land grant he called *Rancho Los Feliz* and led the first Spanish colonists to Los Angeles in 1775.

Griffith J. Griffith, born in Wales in 1850 and rich from mining, purchased the land in 1882. After running an ostrich farm there, he and his wife Tina Mesmer donated 3,015 acres to Los Angeles in 1882. The city gratefully named the park and our mountain after him.

However, the heavy-drinking Griffith shot his wife in the head in 1903. Though disfigured, Mesmer survived. Citing Griffith's "alcoholic insanity," the court convicted him of assault with a deadly weapon instead of attempted murder. Griffith served just two years at San Quentin State Prison. Mesmer obtained a divorce and custody of their son.

Following the scandal, Los Angeles renamed our peak Mount Hollywood, but did not change the park's name. The city also declined further donations Griffith offered until after his death of liver disease in 1919, when it accepted a trust to build the popular theater and observatory that still stand. Mesmer outlived her ex-husband by twenty-nine years, dying in 1948.

MORE MOUNTAIN MATTERS

Some start a Mount Hollywood hike from Charlie Turner Trailhead beside Griffith Observatory. This variation leads through beautiful Berlin Forest, though a parking fee applies and the lot often fills up anyway.

Los Angeles's air quality could stand to improve, but hikers will enjoy the city's cleanest air in the winter months.

Griffith Park contains 4,511 acres in the eastern Santa Monica Mountains, hosting more than 150 plant species, including black walnut trees, found only in the Los Angeles area. Coyotes, foxes, bobcats, and even mountain lions roam the largest historic landmark in Los Angeles. Who knew?

12 RYAN MOUNTAIN

One of the best short hikes in Southern California delivers an unmatched panorama of the surrounding desert and mountains near and far. Climbing Ryan Mountain can impart hikers with a lifelong affinity for Joshua Tree National Park.

Distance: 3 miles round-trip (all on trails)
Time: 2 hours
Difficulty: Class 1; easy to moderate
Land agency: Joshua Tree National Park

Nearest facilities: Twentynine Palms
Trailhead elevation: 4,400 feet
Summit elevation: 5,457 feet
Elevation gain: 1,057 feet
Best season: Oct–May
Permits: None needed

FINDING THE TRAILHEAD

Take Park Boulevard through the national park between the town of Joshua Tree and Twentynine Palms. Find Ryan Mountain Trailhead south of the road, about 3.5 miles east of Hidden Valley Campground, or half a mile west of Sheep Pass Campground.

CLIMBING THE MOUNTAIN

Before hiking, make sure to prepare. This climb delights in fall, winter, and spring but torments hikers in summer, when the park recommends starting no later than seven a.m. Carry adequate water and sun protection in any season, as there is no shade anywhere on the mountain.

Large granite formations stand near the trailhead. In fact, a signed rock shelter shows signs of Native American use dating back centuries and deserves a look. Our path leads south past the boulders and ascends well-placed stone steps. Stay right and south as you pass a junction with a path leading to Sheep Pass Campground.

Joshua trees, cacti, and wildflowers line our path as we steadily climb. As we traverse the northwest ridge, views develop of Hidden Valley and the Wonderland of Rocks below. Our path reveals large and picturesque granite formations on Ryan's west face called Saddle Rocks, a popular rock-climbing area. Keep an eye out for lizards, snakes, and 240 species of birds.

Our climb ends on top of a rounded summit of granite and metamorphic rock, featuring cacti, yucca, and colorful lichen. But most visitors focus on the landscape, including

MORE MOUNTAIN MATTERS

Summer hikers, if they hike at all, should start at first light to avoid dangerously high temperatures.

Joshua trees, the beautiful and unique specimens that inspired the park's name, grow only in the deserts of southeast California, Nevada, Arizona, and Utah. Folklore indicates that Mormon settlers named them for the biblical figure of Joshua, thinking its branches resembled his outstretched arms as he led his people to the Promised Land.

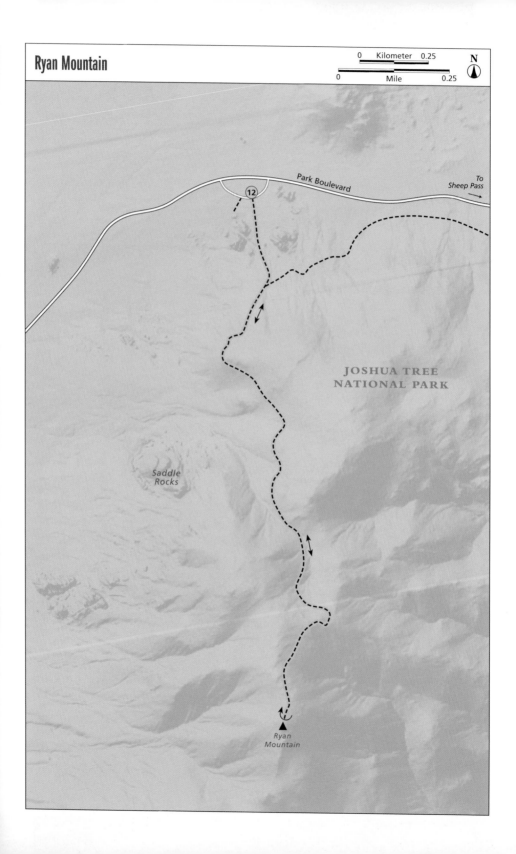

Ryan Mountain

Kilometer
0 — 0.25
Mile
0 — 0.25

N

Park Boulevard
12

To
Sheep Pass

JOSHUA TREE
NATIONAL PARK

Saddle
Rocks

Ryan
Mountain

Spring visitors may spot colorful desert wildflowers like this scarlet hedgehog cactus.

San Jacinto Peak and San Gorgonio Mountain to the west on clear days. Standing closer and within the park are the Little San Bernardino Mountains to the southwest, Pinto Basin and Pinto Mountains to the east, and Queen Mountain to the northeast.

MILES AND DIRECTIONS

0.0   Hike south

0.2   Stay right (south) at trail junction

1.5   Summit

3.0   Arrive back at the trailhead

HIGH HISTORY: PRODUCTIVE PROSPECTOR, PERSISTENT PROTECTOR

A metamorphic rock called Pinto gneiss makes up much of this mountain. Eons of wind and rain have revealed the granite beneath it.

Pinto, Serrano, Cahuilla, Chemehuevi, and Mojave peoples all inhabited this area where the Colorado and Mojave Deserts meet. The Spanish arrived in 1772, and Mexicans explored here in 1823. European American miners and ranchers started operations in the 1860s.

Our mountain's name honors J. D. Ryan, a Montana rancher who in 1895 bought a share of the Lost Horse Mine and helped it become the most profitable in the area. Lost Horse Mine, Lost Horse Well, and the Ryan House still stand as historic ruins nearby.

Conservationist Minerva Hoyt and others campaigned tirelessly for the area's preservation in the 1930s, convincing President Franklin Roosevelt to establish Joshua Tree National Monument in 1936. In appreciation for Hoyt's desert protection efforts, Mexican president Pascual Rubio called her "the Apostle of the Cacti." Congress made Joshua Tree a national park in 1994. The government in 2013 named Mount Minerva Hoyt, which stands about 6 miles northwest of Ryan Mountain.

Echo Mountain

13 ECHO MOUNTAIN

Easily accessible from the Los Angeles area and steeped in both scenery and history, Echo Mountain ranks among the most popular hikes in SoCal. A moderate climb leads to a fascinating summit at the base of the San Gabriel Mountains.

Distance: 5.4 miles round-trip (all on trails)
Time: 3 to 4 hours
Difficulty: Class 1; moderate
Land agency: Angeles National Forest

Nearest facilities: Pasadena
Trailhead elevation: 1,814 feet
Summit elevation: 3,207 feet
Elevation gain: 1,319 feet
Best season: Year-round
Permits: None needed

FINDING THE TRAILHEAD

North of Pasadena in the community of Altadena, drive to the corner of East Loma Alta Drive and North Lake Avenue. Park as close as possible, checking the street signs for restrictions. Our trail begins at the gate of the Cobb Estate.

CLIMBING THE MOUNTAIN

Hike through Cobb Estate, where building foundations remain from this lot's past as a lavish retirement abode. Some call the forest around the estate haunted, but we're too adept in the outdoors for that sort of silliness, right? Don't let the oak trees spook you.

Sam Merrill Trail, named for the Sierra Club member who overhauled and maintained it in the 1940s, leads us through Cobb Estate and up through Las Flores Canyon. Stay right (passing several left-turn options) until the path veers left and crosses Las Flores Creek.

Now the climbing begins in earnest as we ascend switchbacks up the west flank of Echo Mountain. After the final sharp turn, pass three left-turn options to continue south.

At the summit area, we can see track and other remnants of the Mount Lowe Scenic Railway, the first and only electric mountain railway in the United States. Ruins of White City remain, along with interpretive signs explaining the resort's history and demise. To the north stand the San Gabriel Mountains, including Mount Lowe, Brown Mountain, Muir Peak, and Inspiration Point. Look west for Mount Hollywood, Sandstone Peak, and the Pacific Ocean. Greater Los Angeles appears to the south.

MILES AND DIRECTIONS

0.0 From Cobb Estate entrance, hike east on Sam Merrill Trail

0.2 Cross Las Flores Creek

2.7 Summit

5.4 Arrive back at the trailhead

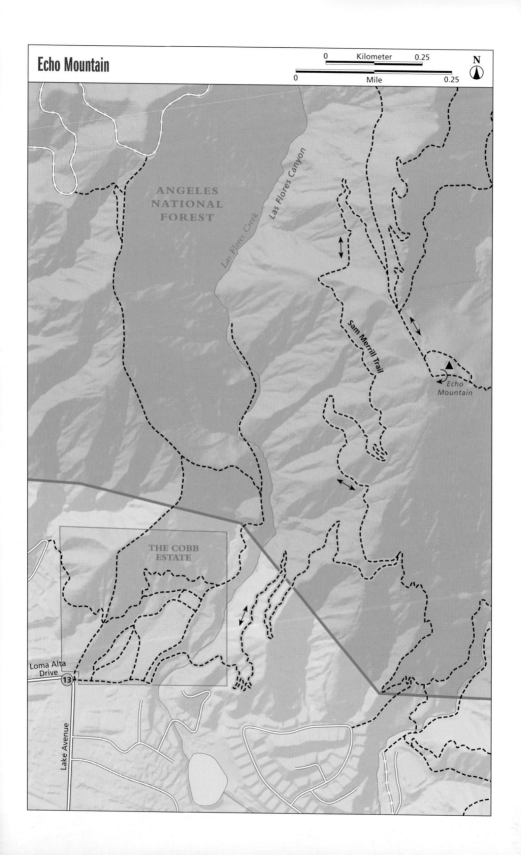

Echo Mountain

ANGELES
NATIONAL
FOREST

Las Flores Creek

Las Flores Canyon

Sam Merrill Trail

Echo
Mountain

THE COBB
ESTATE

Loma Alta
Drive
13

Lake Avenue

0   Kilometer   0.25

0   Mile   0.25

N

Hikers Kacen and Vincent McPhee try out the "echo phone."

HIGH HISTORY: RAILROAD, RESORT, RITZY RESIDENCE, RESIDENTS' RALLY

Mount Lowe Scenic Railway operated from 1893 to 1937, transporting 3 million passengers atop Echo Mountain and its White City resort. In its heyday, the popular tourist area featured a hotel, tennis courts, dance hall, zoo, restaurant, tavern, observatory, and even a miniature golf course. Multiple fires destroyed the resort's buildings in the early twentieth century, leading to the eventual closure of the resort and railway.

Charles and Carrie Cobb bought a 107-acre lot in 1915 and built the Cobb Estate for their retirement home, featuring a Spanish-style mansion. After the Marx Brothers bought it in 1956, the home became a magnet for young misfits and mischief, leading police to arrest hundreds of juveniles there.

When developers prepared to buy the estate in 1971, community members rallied to preserve it. Students of nearby John Muir High School, including Maggie Stratton, teamed up with teacher Bob Barnes and donor Virginia Scott, dramatically buying the property at auction for $175,000 and donating it to the Forest Service.

MORE MOUNTAIN MATTERS

To see why Echo Mountain got its name, try the "echo phone" at the summit pointed north across Castle Canyon.

The name of nearby Mount Lowe honors Thaddeus Lowe (1832–1913), who financed the railway. Earlier, people called it Oak Mountain.

Montecito Peak

14 MONTECITO PEAK

Explore a coastal peak amid the Santa Ynez Mountains overlooking the Pacific Ocean. You may even see a celebrity as you pass through and climb above the affluent neighborhood of Montecito.

Distance: 6-mile loop (all on trails)
Time: 3 to 5 hours
Difficulty: Class 2; moderate
Land agency: Los Padres National Forest
Nearest facilities: Montecito

Trailhead elevation: 750 feet
Summit elevation: 3,214 feet
Elevation gain: 2,464 feet
Best season: Year-round
Permits: None needed

FINDING THE TRAILHEAD

 From Highway 101 just east of Santa Barbara, take exit 94A and drive north on Hot Springs Road. Then turn left onto East Mountain Drive and drive for about a mile. Park in the public area east of Montecito Creek. Find Cold Spring Trailhead up the road to the north.

CLIMBING THE MOUNTAIN

To make a clockwise loop, pass the first right turn that you see and hike north on Cold Spring Canyon Trail as it traces Montecito Creek. Where the trail splits, a sign points us to the East Fork. Oaks that shade our way at first give way to chaparral that carpets these mountains. This first segment of the hike features small waterfalls and holly-leaved cherries.

Soon the trail connects with the loop's eastern side, Cold Spring Ridge Trail, beneath our peak's southwest ridge. Stay left as the segments join to climb the mountain's southwest ridge, which features switchbacks and delivers our first sweeping ocean views. Keep an eye out for a sharp right turn off the main path. This spur trail climbs steeply over rocky ground to the summit.

Rewarding our effort are views of the Santa Ynez Mountains, including Cathedral Peak to the west. Look south to see Santa Barbara, Montecito, the Pacific Ocean, and Santa Cruz Island. Paragliders fly effortlessly overhead on clear days. Sandstone boulders provide convenient seating and invite you to stay a while.

You could return the way you came, but for more variety, complete the loop on the descent. When you return to the junction, turn left instead of right to take the Cold

---

MORE MOUNTAIN MATTERS
Part of our hike passes through 360-acre Gould Park, which Charles and Clara Gould donated to Santa Barbara in 1926.

Hikers can also reach Montecito Peak from Cold Spring Saddle on East Camino Cielo, a 2.3-mile out-and-back variation that actually drops elevation between the trailhead and summit. This is the preferred starting point for cyclists who descend the mountain.

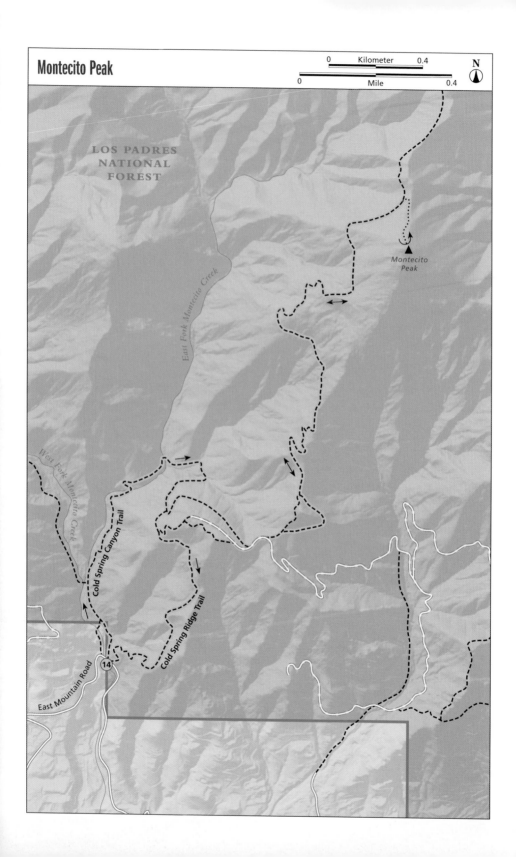

Montecito Peak

LOS PADRES
NATIONAL
FOREST

East Fork Montecito Creek

*Montecito
Peak*

West Fork Montecito Creek

Cold Spring Canyon Trail

Cold Spring Ridge Trail

East Mountain Road

14

N

Spring Ridge Trail. This shorter, steeper variation provides more ocean views than the loop's western side, which we ascended earlier.

If you're hot and weary upon returning from the climb, the pretty beach you viewed from the hike and a refreshing ocean swim are just a few miles away.

MILES AND DIRECTIONS

0.0   Hike north from trailhead

1.3   Stay left (north) at trail junction

2.9   Turn right (south) onto summit spur trail

3.1   Summit

4.8   Turn left (southwest) at trail junction

6.0   Arrive back at the trailhead

HIGH HISTORY: BIG NAMES IN "LITTLE WOODS"

Movements of the Santa Ynez Fault lifted Montecito Peak and its neighboring mountains of the Santa Ynez Range. Chumash Indians occupied this area for more than 10,000 years.

A paraglider flies over Los Padres National Forest.

After the Spanish arrived in 1782, Governor Pedro Fages called it *Montecito*, or "Little Woods." Spanish soldiers and their families settled and built adobe structures, some of which still stand. The nineteenth century saw bandits and outlaws prey upon coastal travelers before large numbers of Italian American farmers arrived in the 1860s.

By the early twentieth century, rich tourists and socialites had built lavish estates. Today the area still attracts wealthy celebrities, such as author Douglas Adams, actor Tom Cruise, television host Ellen DeGeneres, and media magnate Oprah Winfrey.

15 BUTLER PEAK

A moderate hike topped by a historic fire lookout provides an excellent view of Big Bear Lake and its surroundings in San Bernardino National Forest and beyond. Forest roads cover the entire distance, making this an appealing trek for mountain biking.

Distance: 10 miles round-trip (all on forest roads)
Time: 4 to 6 hours
Difficulty: Class 1; moderate
Land agency: San Bernardino National Forest

Nearest facilities: Fawnskin
Trailhead elevation: 7,109 feet
Summit elevation: 8,535 feet
Elevation gain: 1,426 feet
Best season: May–Nov
Permits: None needed

FINDING THE TRAILHEAD

Take Highway 38 north of Big Bear Lake to Fawnskin. Turn north onto Rim of the World Drive (which becomes Forest Road 3N14), drive 1.2 miles to a junction, and park in the limited area beside the road. Forest Road 2N13 starts to the west.

CLIMBING THE MOUNTAIN

When the forest roads are open (typically in summer and fall), high-clearance vehicles can drive within a quarter-mile of the lookout. But you want to hike, right? These directions begin from outside the normal winter road closure.

Follow Forest Road 2N13 to the west. Our route soon curves southwest through a high-desert forest of pines and shrubs.

Near the Hanna Rocks, turn left onto 2N13C. As we gain elevation, views improve of our surroundings, including Grays Peak and Delamar Mountain. We can also see the damage caused by multiple wildfires, as well as the signs of the forest's recovery from them.

Butler Peak with its granite summit crowned by a lookout station comes into clear view when about a half-mile away. Volunteers usually open the lookout to the public between Memorial Day and Labor Day weekends. When it's closed, visitors can still climb up to its balcony.

> **MORE MOUNTAIN MATTERS**
>
> When forest roads allow driving within a stone's throw of the lookout, this outing qualifies as "family-friendly."
>
> Big Bear Lake has provided the setting for many Hollywood films, including *Gone with the Wind* (1939), *Frankenstein* (1931), and *WarGames* (1983).

Highlighting our view are Big Bear Lake and San Gorgonio Mountain to the southeast, and Mount San Antonio and the San Gabriel Mountains to the west. Keep an eye out for bald eagles, as about thirty of them nest near here.

Butler Peak

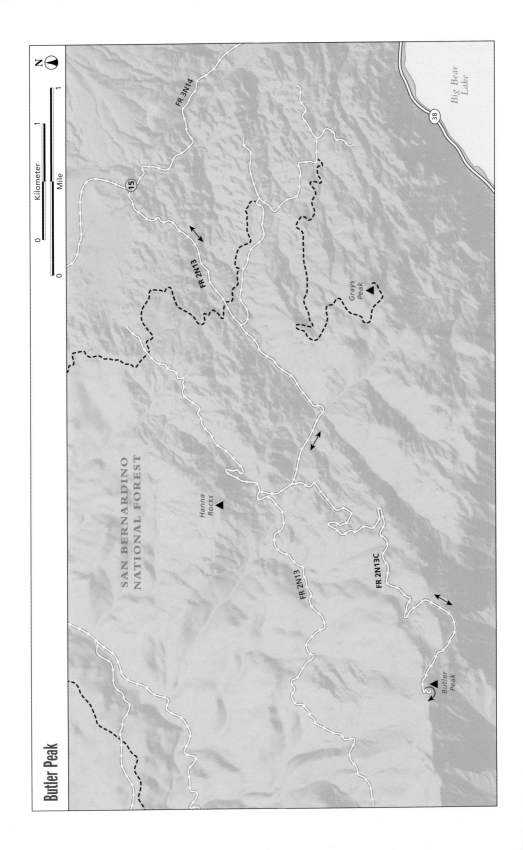

Butler Peak

N

Kilometer
0   1   1

0   1
Mile

SAN BERNARDINO
NATIONAL FOREST

FR 3N14

15

FR 2N13

▲ Grays
  Peak

▲ Hanna
  Rocks

FR 2N13

FR 2N13C

▲ Butler
  Peak

38

Big Bear
Lake

Summit visitors can view Big Bear Lake and San Gorgonio Mountain in San Bernardino National Forest.

MILES AND DIRECTIONS

- **0.0** Hike west on 2N13
- **2.2** Turn left (southwest) at junction onto 2N13C
- **5.0** Summit
- **10.0** Arrive back at the trailhead

HIGH HISTORY: GRIZZLIES AND GOLD, GOING AND GONE

Indigenous people of this area called themselves *Yuhaviatam*, meaning "people of the pines," and the region *Yuhaviat*, which means "pine place." The Spanish called them *Serrano*, meaning "mountain people."

Trapper and trader Benjamin Wilson and his party found the valley while searching for horse thieves in 1845. After they killed and skinned twenty-two grizzlies, they named the area Big Bear Valley. Later others applied the name Big Bear Lake to the nearby small city and reservoir first dammed in 1884, which at the time was the world's largest man-made lake. Miners arrived for a short-lived gold rush starting in 1859. Unregulated hunting of grizzlies drove them to extinction by 1906.

Our mountain's name honors George Butler (1876–1947), a San Bernardino County supervisor and Big Bear Valley property owner. The Civilian Conservation Corps built its lookout station in 1931.

16 CUYAMACA PEAK

Our southernmost outing climbs atop a desert mountain surrounded by a burned but recovering forest. Cuyamaca Peak attracts far fewer people than other moderate SoCal climbs.

Distance: 7.7 miles on a loop (on trails, dirt roads, and paved roads)
Time: 4 to 5 hours
Difficulty: Class 1; moderate
Land agency: Cuyamaca Rancho State Park

Nearest facilities: Julian
Trailhead elevation: 4,852 feet
Summit elevation: 6,512 feet
Elevation gain: 1,834 feet
Best season: Year-round
Permits: None needed

FINDING THE TRAILHEAD

Take Highway 79 into Cuyamaca Rancho State Park and park in the lot beside Paso Picacho Campground and the ranger station (not the visitor center). Find the parking area west of the road, either 11.5 miles north from Highway 8 or 10 miles south from the town of Julian. Azalea Glen Trail leads to the west.

CLIMBING THE MOUNTAIN

Our trail meanders northwest through a young forest. As our path crosses several junctions, follow signs to stay on Azalea Glen Trail. Bedrock mortars prove the long presence of the Kumeyaay here. Middle Peak will stand on your right as we start a counterclockwise loop.

After about a mile, our route curves southwest and starts to gently climb as we approach the base of our mountain. As the climbing begins, views improve of the surrounding peaks and valleys that burned so severely in 2003. Hikers will see abundant evidence of the Cedar Fire but also signs of the forest's recovery. Aided by vigorous reforestation, young oaks, willows, and conifers are sprouting throughout the park.

Watch for a right turn onto Azalea Spring Fire Road and then a left onto Conejos Trail. The path becomes rough and rocky as we climb Cuyamaca Peak's north slope. Turn right as the trail joins Lookout Road for the final approach.

The summit affords perhaps the best view in San Diego County, revealing Mexico, the Pacific Ocean, downtown San Diego, the surrounding Peninsular Ranges, Cleveland National Forest, and summits far beyond it. You could return the way you came, but Lookout Road offers a more-direct return and different scenery, including Stonewall Peak.

MORE MOUNTAIN MATTERS

Cuyamaca Peak collects snow in winter, making cross-country skis or snowshoes helpful.

Our summit marks the second-highest point in San Diego County. Higher by 21 feet is Hot Springs Mountain on Los Coyotes Reservation, but achieving this peak requires a 10-mile round-trip hike and permission from the tribe.

Cuyamaca Peak

MILES AND DIRECTIONS

0.0 Hike west on Azalea Glen Trail

2.2 Turn right (northwest) onto Azalea Spring Fire Road

2.7 Turn left (south) onto Conejos Trail

4.3 Turn right (south) onto Lookout Road

5.0 Summit; return on Lookout Road

7.7 Arrive back at the trailhead

HIGH HISTORY: NATIVE NAME, FEROCIOUS FIRE

Archaeological evidence shows the Kumeyaay people occupied this area for at least 7,000 years. They called the Cuyamaca Mountains *Ah-Ha Kwe-Ah Mac*, meaning "the place where it rains," perhaps because the peaks attract more precipitation than the surrounding desert.

Cuyamaca Peak delivers broad views of Cleveland National Forest.

Cuyamaca Peak

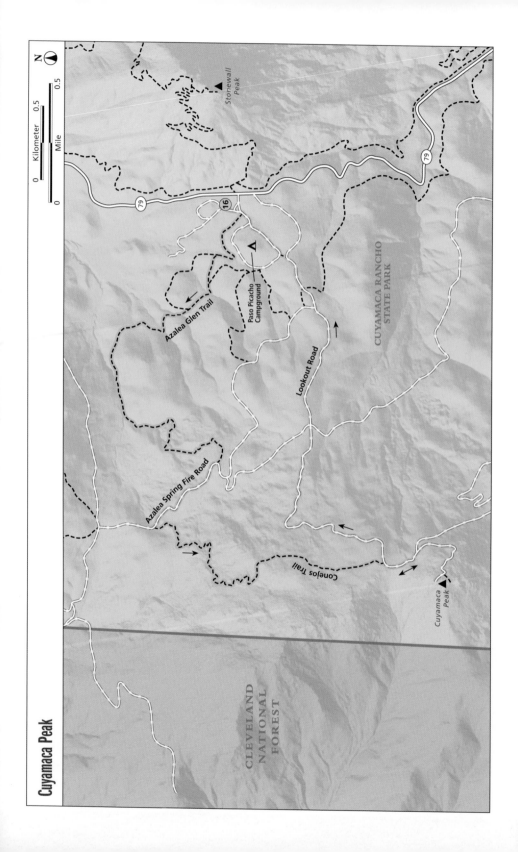

By 1782, the Spanish had arrived and altered the area's indigenous name as "Cuyamaca." Agustin Olvera of Los Angeles obtained the Rancho Cuyamaca grant from the Mexican government in 1845.

The discovery of gold near the town of Julian triggered a frenzied rush in these mountains. Mining continued until 1906.

California bought the rancho property in 1933 for a state park that now includes 26,000 acres. During the Great Depression, Civilian Conservation Corps laborers built campgrounds, trails, and facilities that are still in use.

When a lost hunter lit a signal fire in October 2003, he inadvertently ignited the largest recorded wildfire in California history. The Cedar Fire burned 280,278 acres, including 90 percent of Cuyamaca Rancho State Park, killing 95 percent of the area's conifers. A multiyear reforestation effort to plant more than 1 million seedlings began in 2007. The slow comeback of pine, fir, and oak forests shows more progress every year.

Mount Baden-Powell

17 MOUNT BADEN-POWELL

Mount Baden-Powell packs a lot into a relatively short hike: ancient trees, a historic trail, and a fine summit view featuring both mountains and desert. Boy Scouts who frequently hike on this mountain would tell us to "Be Prepared" (their motto) for a grand adventure.

Distance: 8.2 miles round-trip (all on trails)
Time: 4 to 6 hours
Difficulty: Class 1; moderate
Land agency: Angeles National Forest

Nearest facilities: Big Pines
Trailhead elevation: 6,607 feet
Summit elevation: 9,407 feet
Elevation gain: 2,792 feet
Best season: May–Nov
Permits: None needed

FINDING THE TRAILHEAD

 Take State Route 2 to Vincent Gap. Those near Los Angeles can take State Route 2 east from Glendale. Those closer to Azusa can take State Route 39 north and then turn east on State Route 2. Be advised that State Route 2 west of Vincent Gap usually closes between December and May. Those approaching on State Route 2 west pass through Wrightwood and then drive 5 miles beyond the town of Big Pines. Parking in the trailhead lot requires an Adventure Pass. The trail leads southwest.

CLIMBING THE MOUNTAIN

Find the well-signed trailhead and hike southwest. Our path quickly leads into a forest of oaks, pines, and cedars. Just as quickly, we start a steady climb up the northwest ridge of the mountain. Our route traces both the Pacific Crest Trail (PCT) and the Silver Moccasin Trail, so you might meet some thru-hikers or Boy Scouts along the way.

About forty switchbacks lead to our destination. After about a mile, a bench offers a break and a view. At 1.7 miles, a short side trail leads to Lamel Spring.

Shortly before the summit we enter an area of limber pines, rare trees that live only above 9,000 feet, but for more than 2,000 years. The PCT turns west as our summit trail continues southwest, passing the impressive Wally Waldron Tree, a limber pine named for a Scout leader who helped repair the mountain's trails. The Wally Waldron Tree is estimated to be 1,500 years old and could be the oldest organism in these San Gabriel Mountains.

Our summit view features Mount San Antonio to the southeast, the high desert of Antelope Valley to the north, and the Southern Sierra in the distant northwest. Much closer to the northwest is Devils Punchbowl, a fascinating geologic area where pressure along multiple faults has tilted sandstone into dramatic formations.

MILES AND DIRECTIONS

- 0.0 Hike southwest
- 4.0 At trail junction, turn left (southwest)
- 4.1 Summit
- 8.2 Arrive back at the trailhead

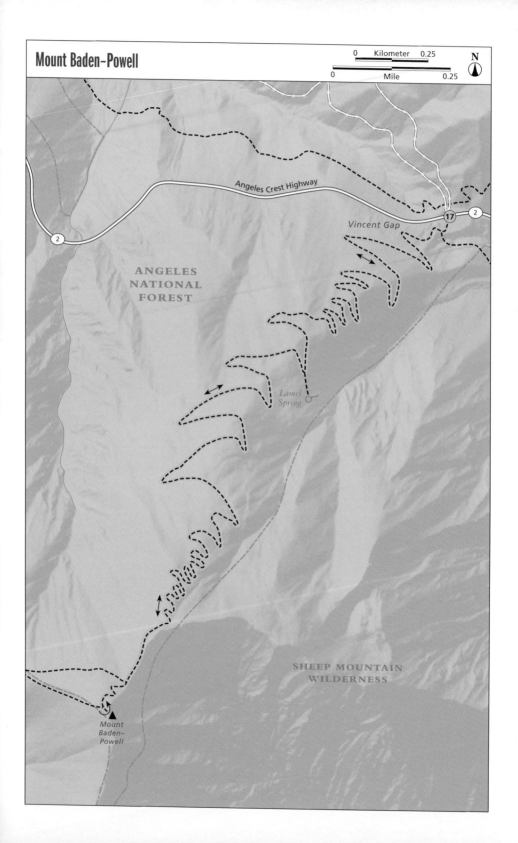

A full moon rises over the summit of Mount Baden-Powell.

HIGH HISTORY: "OUTSTANDING AMONG MOUNTAINS"

Native Americans including the Tongva hiked a trail over this mountain for millennia. Early maps referred to it as East Twin (the other twin being nearby Throop Peak) and North Baldy, in reference to Mount Baldy to the south.

This mountain's current name honors Robert Baden-Powell (1857–1941), the British Army officer who authored *Scouting for Boys* and inspired the international scouting movement. Several thousand people attended a ceremony naming the peak for "The Chief Scout" in 1931. Frederick Burnham declared the peak as "outstanding among mountains as our Chief is among men" at the dedication. The Boy Scouts of America established the 53-mile Silver Moccasin Trail over the mountain in 1942 and placed a marker at the summit honoring Baden-Powell in 1957, the one hundredth anniversary of his birth.

But during the civil rights movement's revival of 2020, critics pointed to the racist writings of both Baden-Powell and Burnham and demanded new names for the mountains that honor the two men.

MORE MOUNTAIN MATTERS

Those interested in extending the adventure can summit Mount Burnham and Throop Peak to the southwest along the PCT and Silver Moccasin Trail. Climbing both and returning to Vincent Gap extends the round-trip distance to about 13 miles.

This trailhead is normally accessible in winter. Climbing the mountain during snow season requires crampons and ice axes. A trail sign rightfully warns of "steep icy slopes" in winter months.

Vincent Gap gets its name from Civil War veteran Tom Vincent, who founded a mine and lived in a cabin near Wrightwood from the 1870s to the 1920s.

Tahquitz Peak

18 **TAHQUITZ PEAK**

Steeped in Native American folklore, Tahquitz Peak stands amid the grand scenery of San Jacinto Wilderness and above the serene surrounding desert. A half-day journey to visit its granite summit will be time well spent.

Distance: 8.2 miles round-trip (all on trails)
Time: 4 to 6 hours
Difficulty: Class 1; moderate
Land agency: San Bernardino National Forest

Nearest facilities: Idyllwild
Trailhead elevation: 6,500 feet
Summit elevation: 8,846 feet
Elevation gain: 2,346 feet
Best season: May–Oct
Permits: Required

FINDING THE TRAILHEAD

 From Idyllwild, take Fern Valley Road to its end at Humber Park Trailhead, which requires an Adventure Pass to park. Find Devil's Slide Trail to the east.

CLIMBING THE MOUNTAIN

Hiking in San Jacinto Wilderness requires a free permit. To get yours, visit San Jacinto Ranger District Office at 54270 Pine Crest in Idyllwild. A quota applies on weekends from Memorial Day through Labor Day; you will need to arrive early to get one on those days.

Aptly named Devil's Slide Trail climbs about 1,700 feet on its way to Saddle Junction. This is a heart-pumping way to start our hike but will get about three-quarters of the elevation gain done early. On the way, keep an eye out for Tahquitz mousetail flowers, which grow only here.

As the terrain flattens at Saddle Junction, turn right onto the Pacific Crest Trail. A pine forest shades our way south toward Chinquapin Flat, where backpackers often camp. At the next trail junction, turn right to leave the PCT and contour southwest past rare limber pines. Soon you'll arrive atop granite Tahquitz Peak, where you will find the highest fire lookout in San Bernardino National Forest.

From the summit, we can unfortunately see the results of the 2018 arson-caused Cranston Fire in San Jacinto Wilderness. But also visible are Marion Mountain, Mount San Antonio, Cuyamaca Peak, many more mountain summits, and vast stretches of high desert.

MILES AND DIRECTIONS

0.0 Hike northeast on Devil's Slide Trail

2.4 Turn right (south) onto Pacific Crest Trail

3.7 Turn right (west) at trail junction

4.1 Summit

8.1 Arrive back at the trailhead

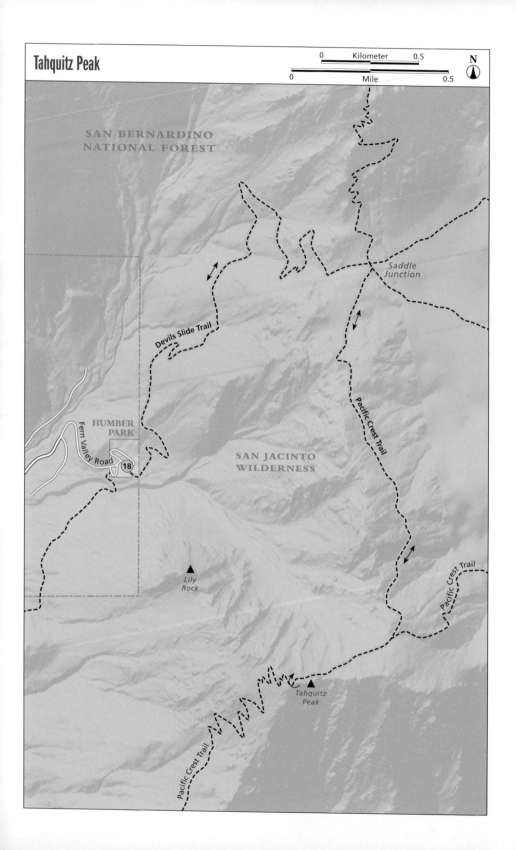

Tahquitz Peak

| 0 | Kilometer | 0.5 |
| 0 | Mile | 0.5 |

N

SAN BERNARDINO
NATIONAL FOREST

Saddle
Junction

Devils Slide Trail

Pacific Crest Trail

HUMBER
PARK

Fern Valley Road

18

SAN JACINTO
WILDERNESS

Lily
Rock

Pacific Crest Trail

Pacific Crest Trail

Tahquitz
Peak

Pacific Crest Trail

Pioneer rock climbers developed modern techniques on Tahquitz Rock.

HIGH HISTORY: DEMON, CHIEF, OR SHAMAN?

Several Native American legends connect to the mountain's name. Some believed Tahquitz was a demon who enjoyed harming and eating people and resided within a large rock. To the Soboba, Tahquitz was a once-beloved chief who was corrupted by evil spirits, leading his tribe to destroy his body even as his spirit escaped to the peak. The Cahuilla tell a similar story, regarding Tahquitz as the first shaman who became selfish and harmful, leading to his banishment in a secret cave. The different tribes seem to agree that Tahquitz's restless spirit causes thunder and other rumblings in the region.

Tahquitz Peak's name appeared on a US Geological Survey (USGS) map in 1901.

Tahquitz Peak Lookout was constructed in 1937 and still operates during the summer and fall.

MORE MOUNTAIN MATTERS

Hikers can also use Devil's Slide Trail and the PCT to access San Jacinto Peak, a challenging climb of about 15 miles round-trip.

Nearby Tahquitz Rock (also known as Lily Rock) and Suicide Rock connect to the United States' earliest technical rock climbing. Sierra Club members and climbing trailblazers, including Royal Robbins, established hundreds of routes there and developed the Yosemite Decimal System, which became the national standard for defining the difficulty of rock-climbing routes.

San Jacinto Peak

19 SAN JACINTO PEAK

Towering over the desert stands the steepest mountain in the Lower 48, but hikers can reach its summit with a surprisingly moderate effort thanks to the Palm Springs Aerial Tramway. Treat yourself to a ride into another world and a unique climbing experience.

Distance: 10 miles round-trip (on trails)
Time: 5 to 7 hours
Difficulty: Class 2; moderate to strenuous (for distance and elevation)
Land agency: Mount San Jacinto State Park

Nearest facilities: Palm Springs
Trailhead elevation: 8,516 feet
Summit elevation: 10,804 feet
Elevation gain: 2,288 feet
Best season: May–Oct
Permits: Required

FINDING THE TRAILHEAD

Find the tram's Valley Station at 1 Tram Way. Hours vary; check its website at pstramway.com. Advance tickets are available and riders can buy tickets on-site. Tram cars normally run every half-hour. The view from the rotating cars alone is worth the price of admission. Exit Mountain Station to the west.

CLIMBING THE MOUNTAIN

Our route starts on a paved path that drops into a forest of pines. Follow the trail leading west that soon reaches a ranger station. Stop here to get a free self-issued wilderness permit. You can also inquire within about trail conditions, especially in winter and spring. Head west when leaving the ranger station and follow signs for San Jacinto Peak.

Mount San Jacinto State Park and the surrounding public lands host more than 250 species of plants and a wide variety of wildlife. We can hope to see bighorn sheep, coyotes, owls, hawks, bobcats, and maybe even a mountain lion.

Our path crosses Long Valley Creek three times and then bends southwest as it climbs toward Round Valley. Overnight hikers with reservations can use the campground here. Continue west and south of the creek to climb to Wellman Divide, where boulders provide seating for a break with a grand view.

Then our route cuts north as it traverses beneath Jean Peak and climbs nearly to the summit of Miller Peak. Another sharp turn takes us beneath the south face of San Jacinto Peak. Near the summit stands a stone hut built by the Civilian Conservation Corps in 1935, which is available for a rest break or emergencies but not for overnight camping. From here the way becomes a bit rocky, but only for a few hundred feet, until the top. Look for the rare limber pines along the way.

"The view from San Jacinto is the most sublime spectacle to be found anywhere on this earth!" wrote naturalist John Muir. Now you can judge for yourself. The summit shows us an incredible variety of Southern California geography, including Joshua Tree National Park, the Mojave Desert, Tahquitz Peak, San Gorgonio Mountain, and dozens of other summits.

San Jacinto Peak

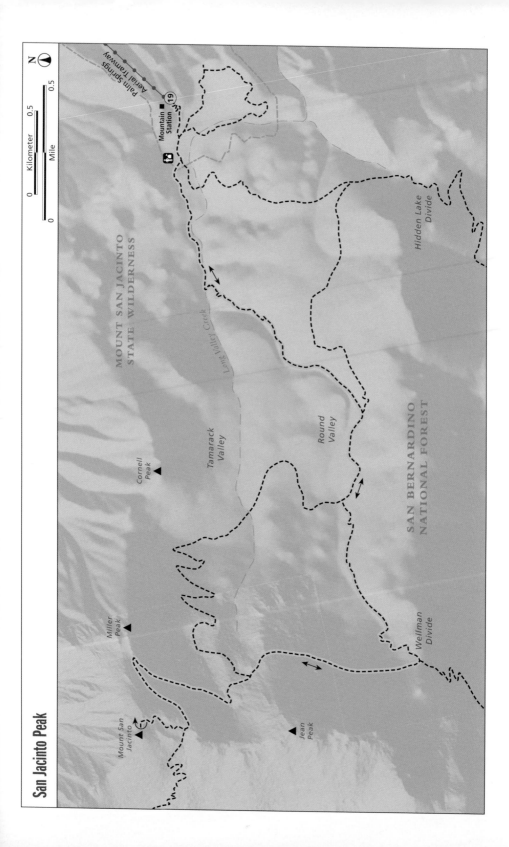

Though desert surrounds the mountain, snow covers San Jacinto Peak's summit.

MILES AND DIRECTIONS

- **0.0** From Mountain Station, hike west
- **0.3** Ranger station (stop for wilderness permit)
- **0.8** Cross Long Valley Creek
- **1.9** Stay left (west) at turnoff to Round Valley Campground
- **3.1** At Wellman Divide, turn right (north)
- **4.9** Stone hut
- **5.0** Summit
- **10.0** Arrive back at the trailhead

HIGH HISTORY: SUMMER SANCTUARY, POLISH PRIEST, GLORIOUS GONDOLAS

San Jacinto Peak stands on the Pacific Plate, which rises as it pushes against the North American Plate at the San Andreas and San Jacinto Faults.

Cahuilla Indians called the mountain *Aya Kaich*, meaning "smooth cliffs," and believed it was the home of their founder, Dakush. They used its upper meadows to escape the desert heat in summer. The Kauisiktum ("people of the fox") occupied a village in Chino Canyon.

The name *San Jacinto* applied to the range on maps by at least 1853. Several Catholic saints share that name; the best known was the Polish priest Hyacinth, who lived from 1185 to 1257. According to a newspaper record, "F. of Riverside" made the first documented ascent in September of 1874. A Wheeler Survey party climbed to its summit in 1878 and named the mountain San Jacinto Peak.

Engineer Francis Crocker first envisioned a tramway to lift people from the desert floor to the high country in 1935. Winning state approval and raising $8 million to finance it took decades. Construction began in 1960 and was completed in 1963; building the supporting towers on perilously steep terrain required extensive use of helicopters. Rotating tramcars debuted in 2000. More than 20 million people have ridden the tramway to ascend 5,873 feet in just ten minutes. It's safe to say that few of them would have ever visited these mountains' upper regions if they had had to make that exhausting climb on their own.

20 MOUNT SAN ANTONIO

Mount San Antonio rates as one of SoCal's most popular hikes for good reason. The mountain which locals affectionately call Mount Baldy provides year-round adventure with multiple options for customized outings. Those standing atop the highest of the San Gabriel Mountains can see Los Angeles yet feel far indeed from California's largest city.

Distance: 10 miles on a loop (on trails and dirt roads)
Time: 6 to 8 hours
Difficulty: Class 2; strenuous (for distance and elevation gain)
Land agency: Angeles National Forest

Nearest facilities: Mount Baldy (village)
Trailhead elevation: 6,159 feet
Summit elevation: 10,064 feet
Elevation gain: 3,905 feet
Best season: April–Nov
Permits: None needed

FINDING THE TRAILHEAD

From Highway 210 between Los Angeles and San Bernardino, take exit 52 to reach Base Line Road and then turn north onto Padua Avenue. Drive 1.8 miles and then turn right onto Mount Baldy Road. Drive 11 miles to Manker Flats, where roadside parking requires an Adventure Pass. The trail begins north of the road.

CLIMBING THE MOUNTAIN

Our journey starts on a paved road that soon passes pretty San Antonio Falls, definitely worth a stop and a look. After a sharp right, the road transitions to gravel. Keep an eye out for a left turn onto Baldy Bowl Trail. The path steepens, but the shade of white fir and pine trees cools our ascent up the mountain's southeast flank.

At 8,300 feet stands the Sierra Club's San Antonio Ski Hut. Built in 1936, the structure shelters overnight travelers with reservations on weekends. Day hikers can take a look, rest on benches outside, and obtain water from a year-round spring.

The trail ascends Baldy Bowl in a clockwise semicircle as it passes through a boulder field and climbs above tree line.

From the summit, we can see the Pacific Ocean, the surrounding San Gabriel Mountains, and dozens of summits in all directions.

The shortest way back simply retraces our steps, but a few extra miles adds variety and provides a gentler descent. For this option, hike east toward Mount Harwood, named for Aurelia Harwood (1865–1928), the first female Sierra Club president. Our trail traverses its southern face, though the ambitious can achieve its 9,538-foot summit with a short detour.

Continue east as our trail climbs over Devils Backbone, a spectacular ridge with sharp drops on either side; avoid this segment when icy. This takes us to Mount Baldy Notch, where a chairlift brings skiers in winter and hikers in summer. A restaurant operates here most weekends. Then simply take the fire road as it descends to the west, passing Manker Canyon, the Baldy Bowl Trail turnoff, and San Antonio Falls before returning us to Manker Flat.

Mount San Antonio

MILES AND DIRECTIONS

0.0 Hike northwest from trailhead

0.6 San Antonio Falls Overlook

0.8 Turn left (north) onto Baldy Bowl Trail

2.5 San Antonio Ski Hut

3.5 Summit; hike east toward Mount Harwood

5.0 Devils Backbone

5.6 Mount Baldy Notch; descend fire road to west

10.0 Arrive back at the trailhead

HIGH HISTORY: NATIVE NAMES, SPANISH SAINT, EXCITING EXPERIMENT

The Tongva called the mountain *Yoát*, meaning "snow," and the Mojave named it *Avii Kwatiinyam*. Spanish missionaries titled it San Antonio after Anthony of Padua, a Franciscan priest and saint. In reference to its treeless summit, European Americans who climbed it in the 1860s gave it the informal name of Mount Baldy. Miners extracted gold for decades in the late nineteenth century.

Mount Harwood neighbors the trail over Devil's Backbone.

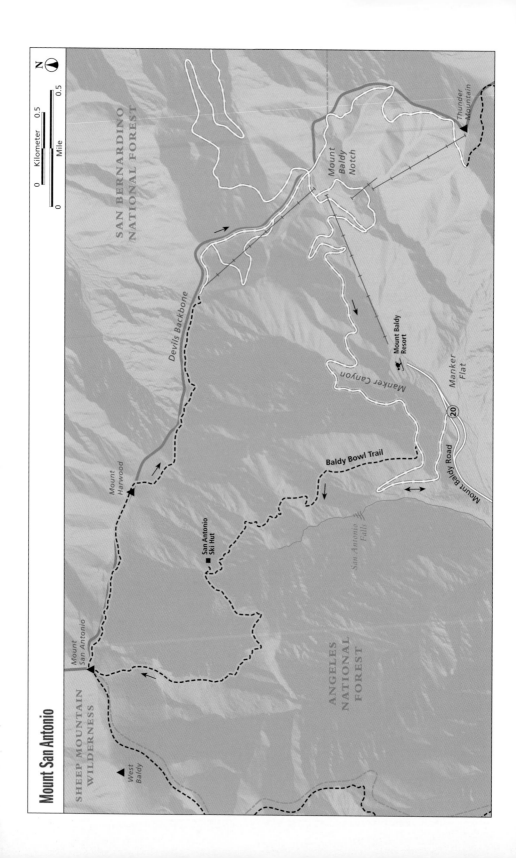

Mount San Antonio

West Baldy ▲

SHEEP MOUNTAIN WILDERNESS

Mount San Antonio ▲

Mount Harwood ▲

San Antonio Ski Hut ■

Devils Backbone

San Antonio Falls

Baldy Bowl Trail

ANGELES NATIONAL FOREST

SAN BERNARDINO NATIONAL FOREST

Mount Baldy Notch

Mount Baldy Resort

Manker Canyon

Manker Flat

20

Mount Baldy Road

Thunder Mountain ▲

N

0   Kilometer   0.5

0   Mile   0.5

Cabins, camps, and resorts sprouted in the early twentieth century as the area became a national forest and a playground for Los Angeles. Though the first ascent is unknown and probably thousands of years in the past, George Bauwens achieved the first documented ascent on skis in 1922. Nobel Prize–winning physicist Albert Michelson performed experiments to measure the speed of light in these mountains from 1922 to 1927. The Civilian Conservation Corps completed Devil's Backbone Trail in 1936. Developed downhill skiing arrived in the 1940s.

MORE MOUNTAINS IN SOCAL

D. THROOP PEAK

Distance: 3 miles round-trip (all on trails)
Time: 1 to 2 hours
Difficulty: Class 1; easy
Land agency: Angeles National Forest
Nearest facilities: Big Pines
Trailhead elevation: 7,901 feet
Summit elevation: 9,138 feet
Elevation gain: 1,237 feet
Best season: May–Nov
Permits: None needed

Throop Peak

This mountain's name honors Amos Throop (1811–1894), who founded Throop College, which became California Institute of Technology in Pasadena. Take State Route 2 west from Big Pines to Dawson Saddle. Climb the trail ascending the ridge to the south of the summit. The peak overlooks the San Gabriel Mountains, including neighboring Mount Lewis, Mount Baden-Powell, and Mount San Antonio.

E. SANDSTONE PEAK

Distance: 3 miles round-trip (all on trails)
Time: 1 to 2 hours
Difficulty: Class 2; moderate
Land agency: Santa Monica Mountains National Recreation Area
Nearest facilities: Thousand Oaks
Trailhead elevation: 2,061 feet
Summit elevation: 3,111 feet
Elevation gain: 1,050 feet
Best season: Year-round
Permits: None needed

Sandstone Peak

Despite its name, Sandstone Peak has volcanic origins and stood more than 10,000 feet high before erosion reduced its elevation by two-thirds. The Chumash people long made their homes near here. A summit plaque honors Boy Scout leader W. Herbert Allen, who donated land for nearby Scout camps. Southwest of Thousand Oaks, take Yerba Buena Road to a signed parking area and trailhead. Out and back is the shortest option, though hikers can also make a rewarding 6-mile loop using the Mishe Mokwa Trail. The summit reveals the surrounding Santa Monica Mountains, the Pacific Ocean, and Santa Cruz Island.

F. KELLER PEAK

Distance: 12.2 miles round-trip (on trails and a forest road)
Time: 6 to 8 hours
Difficulty: Class 1; moderate
Land agency: San Bernardino National Forest
Nearest facilities: Arrowbear Lake
Trailhead elevation: 6,027 feet
Summit elevation: 7,882 feet
Elevation gain: 1,855 feet
Best season: May–Nov
Permits: None needed

Keller Peak

This peak and lookout built in 1926 are named for Forest Service employee Ally Keller (1868–1942). A B-26 bomber crashed into the mountain in 1941, killing all nine crew members. Take Highway 18 between Running Springs and Arrowbear Lake, turn south onto Keller Peak Road, and park at the first opportunity. Take Exploration Trail 4.4 miles to the east and then take Keller Peak Road south to the lookout. From the summit we can see Butler, San Bernardino, San Jacinto, Tahquitz, Cuyamaca, and Sandstone peaks, as well as the Pacific Ocean. Visitors can customize shorter hikes by driving closer to the mountain when the road is open in summer and fall. Cyclists can use Keller Peak Road.

Lake Tahoe's Emerald Bay

Yosemite Valley

SIERRA NEVADA

Students of Mount Tallac Continuation High School thought little about the nearby peak that inspired their school's name. That changed when their principal marched them up to the 9,735-foot summit overlooking Lake Tahoe in 2014.

The 10-mile adventure that climbs 3,255 feet up Mount Tallac has inspired hundreds of the school's students since then.

"It's similar to the journey of life, 'cause you get started and you're so excited," shared former student Tucker Leonard. "Thirty minutes in, you're sweating and struggling, asking yourself why, until you reach the first lake. Then you're stoked. You realize what you are doing is a blessing and beautiful experience."

Later, "you are feeling exhausted up the steep long stretch to the top," recalled Leonard. "Once you get to the top, you realize you pushed through to make it and the feeling of accomplishment and happiness overwhelms you."

Rich experiences and scenery fill the western side of the Sierra Nevada. California's largest mountain range runs about 400 miles long, with a national monument, three national parks, and eight national forests.

Grinding tectonic plates raised the range, glaciers carved its canyons, and streams and rivers carry sediment from the mountains to the Central Valley. Though the range shows some volcanic activity, ice-carved granite dominates the landscape in places like Yosemite.

The Sierra's western slope drops more gently than its eastern flank, making it more accessible and thus, more frequently visited. Highways 80, 50, and 88 remain open year-round, except during heavy storms. Highways 4, 108, and 120 are closed at high elevations each winter, usually reopening in May or June.

Most of this section's summits make suitable climbs in summer and fall. A few outings also beckon in winter and spring, like Mount Tallac.

After the students' first ascent, Principal Holly Greenough made the climb an annual event. Teens who never hiked before celebrating on the summit became a yearly highlight.

"They come back feeling really accomplished, surprised at what they were able to do, and very proud of themselves," said Greenough, a third-generation Lake Tahoe educator. "There's true power and beauty in standing on top of the mountain. It teaches kids and adults far more than any classroom lesson."

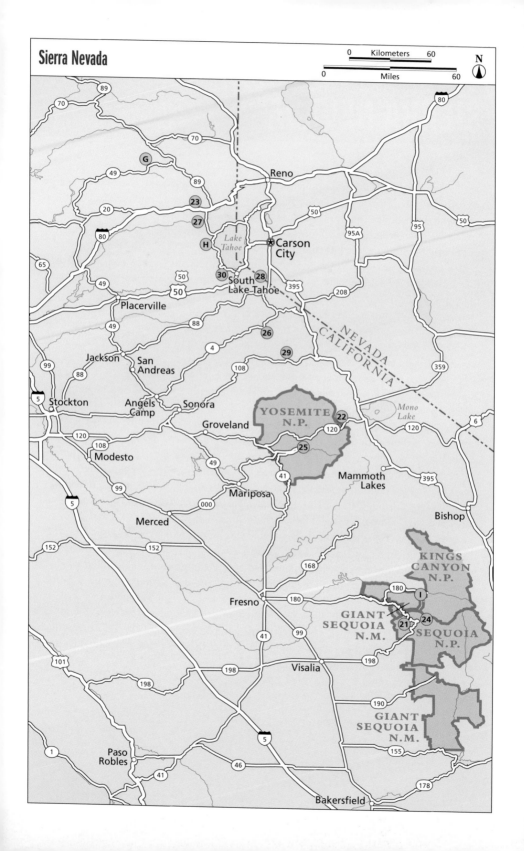

Sierra Nevada

0 Kilometers 60
0 Miles 60

N

89
70
70
89
G
49
89
Reno
23
20
27
50
80
H
Lake
Tahoe
95A
95
50
65
50
30
28
South
Lake Tahoe
395
208
Carson
City
49
50
50
Placerville
88
26
49
88
Jackson
4
29
San
Andreas
108
NEVADA
CALIFORNIA
359
99
Stockton
Angels
Camp
Sonora
Mono
Lake
6
5
120
YOSEMITE
N.P.
22
Groveland
120
120
108
25
Modesto
49
Mammoth
Lakes
395
99
41
Mariposa
000
Merced
Bishop
5
152
152
KINGS
CANYON
N.P.
168
Fresno
180
180
I
GIANT
SEQUOIA
N.M.
24
41
99
21
SEQUOIA
N.P.
198
101
Visalia
198
198
190
GIANT
SEQUOIA
N.M.
5
155
1
Paso
Robles
46
41
178
Bakersfield

Sierra Nevada Peaks at a Glance

SUMMIT	DISTANCE	DIFFICULTY	LAND AGENCY	SUMMIT ELEVATION	ELEVATION GAIN	BEST SEASON
21. Little Baldy	3.2 miles	Class 1; easy	Sequoia National Park	8,044 feet	709 feet	June–Oct
22. Gaylor Peak	2 miles	Class 2; easy to moderate	Yosemite National Park	11,004 feet	1,061 feet	July–Oct
23. Mount Judah	5.2 miles	Class 1; moderate	Tahoe National Forest	8,243 feet	1,133 feet	June–Oct
24. The Watchtower	6.6 miles	Class 2; moderate	Sequoia National Park	8,973 feet	1,693 feet	June–Oct
25. North Dome	9.6 miles	Class 1; moderate	Yosemite National Park	7,542 feet	-608 feet	June–Nov
26. Hiram Peak	2.6 miles	Class 2; moderate	Stanislaus National Forest	9,795 feet	1,165 feet	June–Oct
27. Granite Chief	10 miles	Class 2; moderate	Tahoe National Forest	9,006 feet	2,776 feet	June–Oct
28. Jobs Peak	4.4 miles	Class 1; strenuous	Humboldt-Toiyabe National Forest	10,663 feet	2,063 feet	June–Oct
29. Stanislaus Peak	8 miles	Class 2; strenuous	Stanislaus National Forest	11,233 feet	1,801 feet	June–Oct
30. Mount Tallac	9.6 miles	Class 2; strenuous	Lake Tahoe Basin Management Unit	9,735 feet	3,255 feet	June–Oct
G. Sierra Buttes	4.6 miles	Class 1; moderate	Tahoe National Forest	8,587 feet	1,587 feet	June–Oct
H. Ellis Peak	6.2 miles	Class 1; moderate	Tahoe National Forest	8,740 feet	1,667 feet	June–Oct
I. Lookout Peak	10.4 miles	Class 3; strenuous	Kings Canyon National Park	8,531 feet	3,861 feet	June–Oct

Little Baldy

21 LITTLE BALDY

A short and pleasant jaunt leads to the top of a modest summit with a fine panoramic view of Sequoia National Park. This is a perfect first climb for kids, beginners, recent arrivals to high elevation, and those working up to longer outings. Little Baldy gets much less visitation than other Sequoia attractions like General Sherman Tree and Moro Rock.

Distance: 3.2 miles round-trip (all on trails)
Time: 2 to 3 hours
Difficulty: Class 1; easy
Land agency: Sequoia National Park
Nearest facilities: Wuksachi Village

Trailhead elevation: 7,335 feet
Summit elevation: 8,044 feet
Elevation gain: 709 feet
Best season: June–Oct
Permits: None needed

FINDING THE TRAILHEAD

Park at Little Baldy Saddle beside Generals Highway, either 5 miles northwest of Wuksachi Village or 1.5 miles south of Dorst Creek Campground.

CLIMBING THE MOUNTAIN

Our trail begins on the east side of the road, leads northeast, and climbs gradually. The path is occasionally rocky but well-traveled and easy to follow. We pass through an old-growth forest that eventually transitions into a young and dense forest of short pines. A wide variety of wildflowers grows along the way. Keep an eye out for wildlife, as well; hikers often spot grouse, marmot, deer, and bear here.

Views improve as the elevation increases. A false summit offers a glimpse through the trees at distant landscapes, but don't be fooled. Walk a little farther and you will emerge from the trees atop a large granite dome. The trail has no clear ending, but you'll know you're on the summit when you see clear views of the High Sierra to the east and San Joaquin Valley to the west.

MILES AND DIRECTIONS

0.0   Hike northeast on Little Baldy Trail

0.5   Stay on Little Baldy Trail as it makes switchbacks and turns south

1.6   Summit

3.2   Arrive back at the trailhead

HIGH HISTORY: WINDY WAY, PRICEY PAVEMENT

This peak overlooks Generals Highway, a steep and winding 46-mile road that connects Kings Canyon and Sequoia National Parks. Construction began in 1921 and concluded in 1935, costing a then-hefty sum of $2.25 million. The road's name refers to General

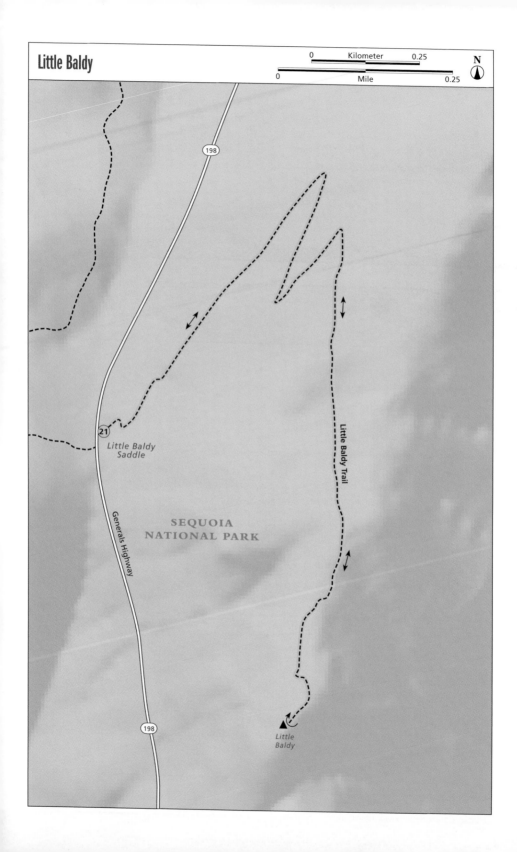

Little Baldy

Kilometer
0   0.25
Mile
0   0.25

N

198

21

Little Baldy
Saddle

Generals Highway

Little Baldy Trail

SEQUOIA
NATIONAL PARK

198

Little
Baldy

For a short hike, Little Baldy provides a big view of Sequoia National Park.

Grant Tree in Kings Canyon National Park and General Sherman Tree in Sequoia National Park.

MORE MOUNTAIN MATTERS

With its open view to the west, Little Baldy makes a great spot to view and photograph the sunset.

If you like Little Baldy, then you may also enjoy Big Baldy, a slightly taller peak that also lacks "hair." Find its trailhead on Generals Highway about 12 miles north of Little Baldy Saddle. A 4.4-mile hike leads to the summit and back.

Gaylor Peak

22 GAYLOR PEAK

Starting from a high pass, hiking only a mile and gaining just over 1,000 feet, this might be the easiest 11,000-footer that you ever climb on the right day. Add a scenic view and an interesting history and Gaylor Peak has all the elements of a short but enjoyable adventure.

Distance: 2 miles round-trip (on trails and use trails)
Time: 1 to 2 hours
Difficulty: Class 2; easy to moderate
Land agency: Yosemite National Park

Nearest facilities: Tuolumne Meadows
Trailhead elevation: 9,943 feet
Summit elevation: 11,004 feet
Elevation gain: 1,061 feet
Best season: July–Oct
Permits: None needed

FINDING THE TRAILHEAD

Park in the lot on the north side of Highway 120 just west of the Tioga Pass entrance station. If the lot is full, you can also park beside the highway just east of the entrance station.

CLIMBING THE MOUNTAIN

Take the signed trail toward Gaylor Lakes and start your brisk climb through scattered and hardy whitebark and lodgepole pines.

Hikers will reach a pass between Gaylor Peak and the Gaylor Lakes after half a mile. Turn off the well-traveled trail to the lake and instead follow a use trail toward the right. You'll reach the summit after another half-mile.

From here you'll see features including Middle Gaylor Lake, Granite Lakes, Lee Vining Canyon, Mount Dana, the Cathedral Range, and much more.

If you're ready for a little more adventure before returning, the trail to Middle Gaylor Lake, around it, and back to the saddle adds just 1.3 miles to your outing. That's where to go for the best pictures of Gaylor Peak.

MORE MOUNTAIN MATTERS

Though this outing is short in both distance and elevation gain, the high elevation of the starting point and summit make this a better choice for those who have spent a few days in the mountains than for those who just drove up from sea level.

Gaylor Peak makes a nice snowy adventure for cross-country skiers and snowshoers soon after Tioga Road opens to automobiles in May or June.

Anglers report good fishing at Gaylor and Granite Lakes.

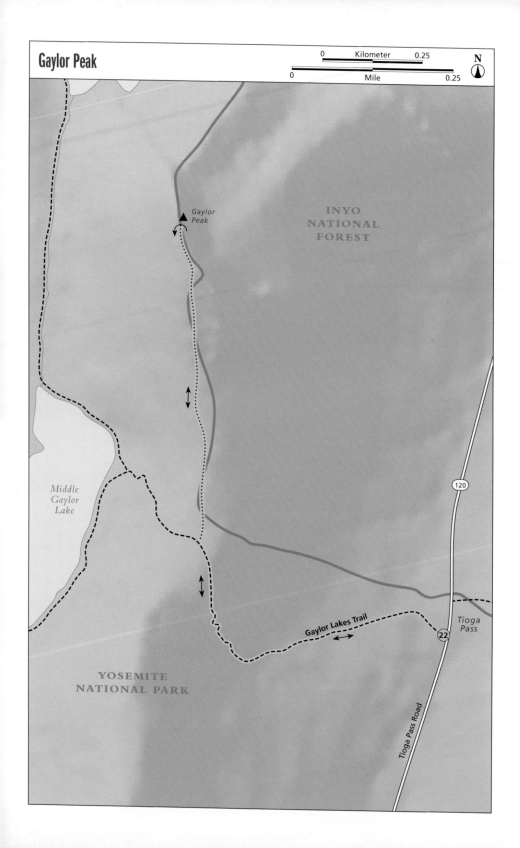

Gaylor Peak

0   Kilometer   0.25

0   Mile   0.25

N

INYO
NATIONAL
FOREST

*Gaylor
Peak*

*Middle
Gaylor
Lake*

120

Gaylor Lakes Trail

22

*Tioga
Pass*

YOSEMITE
NATIONAL PARK

Tioga Pass Road

Gaylor Peak stands over Tioga Pass and the Yosemite high country.

MILES AND DIRECTIONS

0.0   From Tioga Pass parking area, hike west on Gaylor Lakes Trail

0.5   At the pass, leave Gaylor Lakes Trail and turn right (north) onto a use trail

1.0   Summit

2.0   Arrive back at the trailhead

HIGH HISTORY: ROVING RANGER'S REALM

During the mining days of the Tioga Pass area, prospectors knew the peak as "Tioga Hill." But now it carries the name of Andrew Jack Gaylor (1846–1921), one of the first Yosemite rangers for his last fourteen years of life. Gaylor had also served as a civilian packmaster during the Spanish-American War. Before shipping out with the Rough Riders, he wrote these words of advice to his son: "Love many, trust few, and always paddle your own canoe."

Mount Judah

23 MOUNT JUDAH

Scenery and history combine on a moderate and popular loop trail. Climb among summits of Tahoe National Forest that saw Native American settlements, the Donner Party, and the first transcontinental railroad.

Distance: 5.2 miles on a loop (all on trails)
Time: 2 to 3 hours
Difficulty: Class 1; moderate
Land agency: Tahoe National Forest
Nearest facilities: Truckee

Trailhead elevation: 7,110 feet
Summit elevation: 8,243 feet
Elevation gain: 1,133 feet
Best season: June–Oct
Permits: None needed

FINDING THE TRAILHEAD

 From Interstate 80 about 13 miles east of Truckee, take the Soda Springs–Norden exit and turn east onto Donner Pass Road. Drive 3.5 miles to Donner Pass. Park in a lot south of the road (or beside nearby Lake Mary Road).

CLIMBING THE MOUNTAIN

Hike southwest on the Pacific Crest Trail as it briefly overlaps Old Donner Summit Road. The nearby railroad tunnels are the work of Chinese American laborers who toiled for years to blast through solid granite in the 1860s.

Turn left (southeast) to stay on the PCT as the trail parts from the road. Follow the trail as it climbs up switchbacks through a granite boulder field. You will gain a view of Summit Camp, once home to the Chinese American railroad workers.

Climbing eases as the trail continues south and leads to the Mount Judah Loop junction. Turn left (north) to start the loop in a clockwise direction. Keep a lookout for the rugged junipers, which can exceed 3,000 years of age.

As the loop turns south, you will pass a side trail to the top of Donner Peak. Gaining this bonus summit adds less than 0.5 mile to your outing.

After a few more switchbacks, our trail traces the ridge leading to the summit, affording a view of Donner Lake, Mount Lincoln, and Anderson Peak.

Hikers can retrace their steps to descend or complete the loop; either way amounts to nearly the same distance. To finish the loop, hike down the mountain's southwest ridge until it rejoins the PCT and turn right (northeast). Follow the trail along Mount Judah's western flank. On this segment you might spot Sierra Crest signs affixed to trees, used to mark cross-country ski trails established in the 1930s.

When you reach the next trail junction, you have completed the loop. Turn left (north) to retrace the first trail segment and return to the parking lot.

MILES AND DIRECTIONS

0.0 Hike southeast from parking lot on Old Donner Summit Road / Pacific Crest Trail

0.1 Turn left (southeast) to stay on PCT

Mount Judah hikers enjoy views of Anderson Peak and Tinker Knob in Tahoe National Forest.

1.0 Turn left (north) onto Mount Judah Loop

1.7 Turn right (southwest) at trail junction to stay on loop trail (or make northeast detour to Donner Peak)

2.6 Summit; continue southwest to stay on loop trail

3.3 Turn right (northeast) as loop trail rejoins PCT

4.2 Stay left (north) to stay on PCT

5.2 Arrive back at the trailhead

HIGH HISTORY: DONNER DISASTER, INSIGHTFUL ENGINEER, CHINESE CONSTRUCTION

Native Americans traveled and summered in the Donner Pass area for thousands of years, leaving behind petroglyphs, grinding mortars, and arrowheads.

European Americans' first wagon trains to California passed through in 1844. The Donner Party followed their route to disaster in 1846, as an early winter trapped the group for months, leading dozens to starve and freeze to death.

MORE MOUNTAIN MATTERS

Donner Peak (8,019 feet) makes a nice detour and bonus peak from the loop's northeast curve, adding less than 0.5 mile to the outing.

Cross-country skiers and snowshoers enjoy ascending Mount Judah in the right conditions. When approaching from Old Donner Summit Road, the base of the mountain is among the steeper sections, but the climbing eases after that.

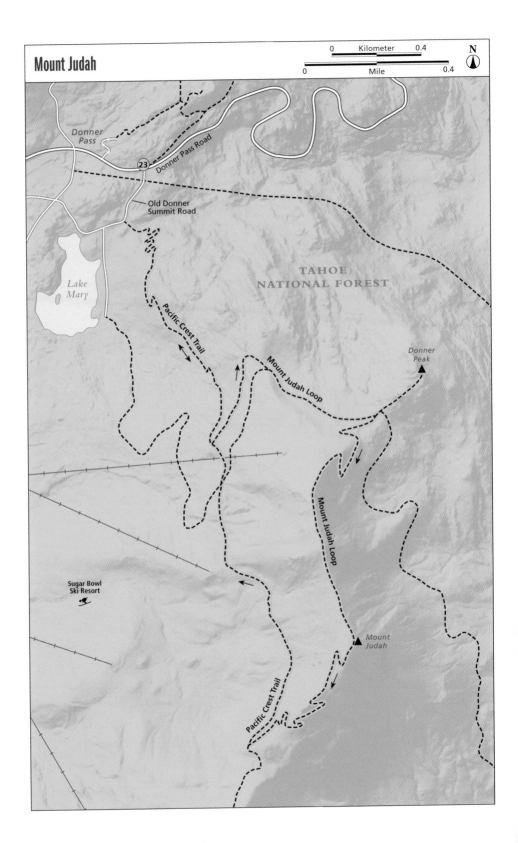

Mount Judah

Donner
Pass

23 Donner Pass Road

Old Donner
Summit Road

Lake
Mary

TAHOE
NATIONAL FOREST

Pacific Crest Trail

Mount Judah Loop

Donner
Peak

Mount Judah Loop

Sugar Bowl
Ski Resort

Mount
Judah

Pacific Crest Trail

0   Kilometer   0.4

0   Mile   0.4

N

This mountain's name honors Theodore Judah (1826–1863), an engineer who promoted the first transcontinental railroad. Judah surveyed the Sierra Nevada for the best route over the mountains. Some considered such a project impossible, calling him "Crazy Judah," but Chinese American laborers employed by Central Pacific Railroad concluded the exhausting and dangerous construction in 1869. Judah died of yellow fever six years earlier, at just 37 years of age. The route he surveyed remained in use until 1993, near the peak that now bears his name. This area also saw the Lincoln Highway, the nation's first transcontinental road for automobiles.

24 THE WATCHTOWER

This moderate outing leads through a vibrant forest to a dramatic and fascinating mountaintop at the edge of a beautiful and popular cluster of backcountry lakes.

Distance: 6.6 miles round-trip (on trails with some rock scrambling)
Time: 3 to 4 hours
Difficulty: Class 2; moderate
Land agency: Sequoia National Park
Nearest facilities: Lodgepole Village

Trailhead elevation: 7,280 feet
Summit elevation: 8,973 feet
Elevation gain: 1,693 feet
Best season: June–Oct
Permits: None needed

FINDING THE TRAILHEAD

From Generals Highway in Sequoia National Park, turn northeast onto Wolverton Road and drive about 1.5 miles to Wolverton Picnic Area.

CLIMBING THE MOUNTAIN

Hike north from the parking lot to a trail junction. Turn toward the right (northeast) to stay on Lakes Trail. Hike east beside Wolverton Creek on the path through a forest of pines and firs. Turn left (north) at the next trail junction toward Heather Lake and Pear Lake. Now the climbing becomes steeper.

Our next junction offers a choice of the Watchtower Trail or the Hump Trail; stay left for the Watchtower. From here to the peak is another 1.3 miles, crossing seasonal creeks. Look for corn lilies, ranger's buttons, and columbine wildflowers along the way.

Watchtower's granite summit stands across a chasm north of the trail. Most passersby are content to admire it from the trailside. Some scamper up Class 2 terrain on its southwest flank, but be advised that its north and east faces drop more than 1,000 feet, with no fencing or rails. Parents beware: Although many children hike this trail, the summit is no place for kids. Admire Tokopah Valley and the Marble Fork of the Kaweah River to the north.

MORE MOUNTAIN MATTERS

To make a longer trip and a loop, continue to Heather Lake and return via the Hump Trail for a total distance of about 8 miles. This way you'll get to see the most dramatic portion of the trail (between the Watchtower and Heather Lake), where CCC workers blasted into the solid granite of the mountainside.

If you wish to camp, excellent sites are found farther up the trail beside Emerald and Pear Lakes (permit required). There is no camping allowed at Aster or Heather Lakes.

Although Wolverton is a popular winter recreation area, the park closes the Watchtower Trail when icy or snowed over, for safety reasons. Do not attempt this hike in winter or wet conditions; fatalities have occurred on the steep cliffs.

The Watchtower

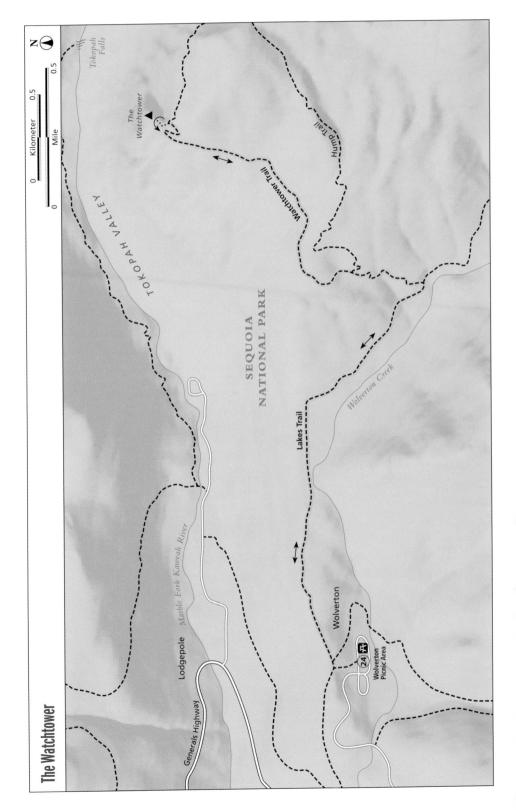

The Watchtower's steep and dangerous edges demand great caution.

MILES AND DIRECTIONS

0.0 Hike north on Lakes Trail

0.1 Turn right (northeast) at junction to stay on Lakes Trail

1.7 Turn left (north) at junction toward Heather Lake and Pear Lake

2.0 Stay left (north) for the Watchtower Trail

3.3 Summit

6.6 Arrive back at the trailhead

HIGH HISTORY: NATIVE NAME, TENDER-AGED TRAILBLAZERS

Both Tokopah Falls and Tokopah Valley get their names from a Yokut term for "high mountain valley." This mountain's steep and pointy appearance as seen from Tokopah Falls inspired its informal name; most maps do not identify it except as an unnamed 8,973-foot peak.

More than 1,100 members of FDR's Civilian Conservation Corps worked in and around Sequoia National Park starting in 1933. Some of the young men camped at nearby Emerald Lake while working on this trail, earning $1 a day each for their labor.

25 NORTH DOME

Here's a rare mountain with a summit lower than its trailhead, but climbers who achieve it will still feel on top of the world as they look down on Yosemite Valley. The moderate hike includes some gentle ups and downs and an optional detour to the interesting Indian Rock formation. North Dome's summit boasts the best views of Half Dome and Clouds Rest in the park.

Distance: 9.6 miles round-trip (all on trails)
Time: 4 to 6 hours
Difficulty: Class 1; moderate (for distance)
Land agency: Yosemite National Park

Nearest facilities: Tuolumne Meadows
Trailhead elevation: 8,150 feet
Summit elevation: 7,542 feet
Elevation gain: -608 feet
Best season: June–Nov
Permits: None needed

FINDING THE TRAILHEAD

Park beside Highway 120 at Porcupine Creek trailhead; don't confuse this with Porcupine Flat Campground a mile to the west.

CLIMBING THE MOUNTAIN

Our trail to the south leads over an old paved road for the first 0.7 mile, through fern-filled meadows and across Porcupine Creek. This is the last reliable source of water until you return here. You will pass a few trail junctions in the first 2 miles. Simply follow the signs for North Dome through the forest of Jeffrey pines and lodgepole pines. At about 2.8 miles, a trail sign and junction appear for Indian Rock, a natural arch formation atop a hill 0.3 mile to the northeast. This is a worthy detour, but afternoon light makes it more photogenic, so you may want to check it out on your return trip.

Continuing south, the forest thins and gives way to granite slabs. Be alert because the trail here is harder to follow than the path through the trees, but it's still fairly clear as long as it's free of snow.

Soon North Dome itself comes into view and our trail leads us down into a small gully beside it before climbing the final steps to its summit. From here you can look over much of Yosemite Valley and Tenaya Canyon, and Half Dome appears close enough to touch.

> **MORE MOUNTAIN MATTERS**
>
> Some think Chief Tenaya's face appears on the southwest face of Clouds Rest. North Dome's summit is the best place to see this. Light and shadow make it most visible on clear days from mid-morning to noon.
>
> Sunlight illuminates the sheer face of Half Dome from mid-afternoon to early evening on clear days.

North Dome

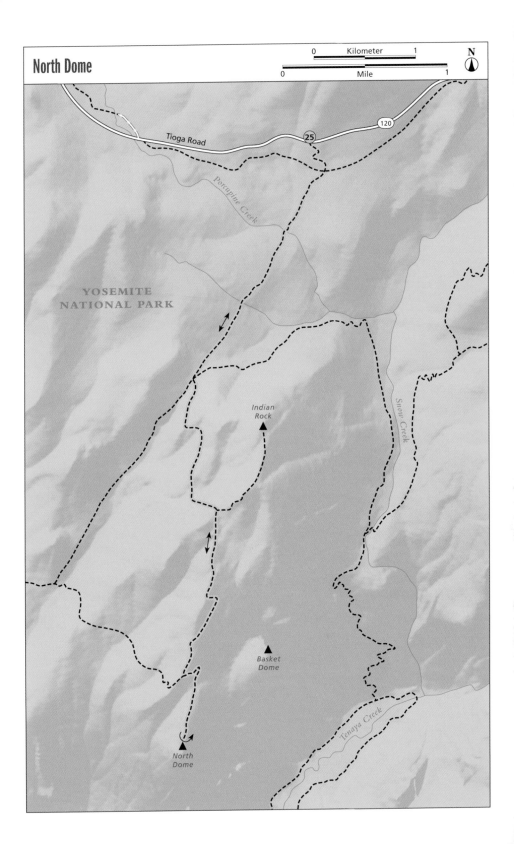

North Dome

Kilometer

Mile

N

Tioga Road

120

25

Porcupine Creek

YOSEMITE
NATIONAL PARK

Indian
Rock

Snow Creek

Basket
Dome

Tenaya Creek

North
Dome

Indian Rock frames a unique Half Dome view.

MILES AND DIRECTIONS

0.0 Hike southwest from Porcupine Creek trailhead

1.7 Stay right (south) at Snow Creek trail junction

1.8 Turn left (south) at Yosemite Falls trail junction

2.8 Stay right (south) at Indian Rock trail junction

4.8 Summit

9.6 Return to start

HIGH HISTORY: GLACIER-CARVED GRANITE, SPIRIT'S STONY SENTENCE

Glaciers and rivers carved North Dome and other granite formations of Yosemite Valley over eons.

The Ahwahneechee believed their Great Spirit had punished a husband and wife for "wickedness" and turned them both into stone. According to legends, the man Nan-gas became the mountain now called North Dome, the woman Tis-si-ak became Half Dome, and the basket she threw at her husband in anger became nearby Basket Dome.

26 HIRAM PEAK

A high trailhead makes a short hike feel like a High Sierra adventure, complete with an astounding panoramic view. This climb gives you a good reason to get off the main highway and discover the attractive Highland Lakes area.

Distance: 2.6 miles round-trip (on trails and use trails)
Time: 1 to 2 hours
Difficulty: Class 2; moderate
Land agency: Stanislaus National Forest

Nearest facilities: Bear Valley
Trailhead elevation: 8,630 feet
Summit elevation: 9,795 feet
Elevation gain: 1,165 feet
Best season: June–Oct
Permits: None needed

FINDING THE TRAILHEAD

Take Highland Lakes Road leading southeast from Highway 4—about 4 miles east from Hermit Valley Campground if eastbound, or 1.3 miles west of Ebbetts Pass if westbound. Drive the paved and dirt road (generally passable for low-clearance vehicles) for 5.8 miles to Highland Lakes Campground beside the second and smaller lake. Our hike begins to the southeast.

CLIMBING THE MOUNTAIN

Hike southeast beside Upper Highland Lake and make a quick left toward the campground. The route quickly climbs above tree line to a plateau beneath the summit. Then the final approach ascends a rocky slope on the mountain's north face.

Our summit view features mountains of Mokelumne and Carson-Iceberg Wildernesses. Nearby summits of Airola, Iceberg, and Folger Peaks could be within your reach today if you want to extend your outing. More-distant challenges include Highland, Stanislaus, and Sonora Peaks.

MILES AND DIRECTIONS

0.0   Hike southeast beside Upper Highland Lake

0.1   Turn left toward campground and follow the trail as it curves right (southeast)

0.6   Turn right (south) at trail junction

1.3   Summit

2.6   Arrive back at the trailhead

HIGH HISTORY: SNOWSTORM, STEAMBOAT, AND "SNOWSHOE"

Miwuk and Washoe Indians first traveled the Ebbetts Pass corridor. Jedediah Smith and his party in 1827 became the first non-natives to crest the Sierra Nevada near here, surviving a fierce snowstorm that killed some of their pack animals.

Hiram Peak

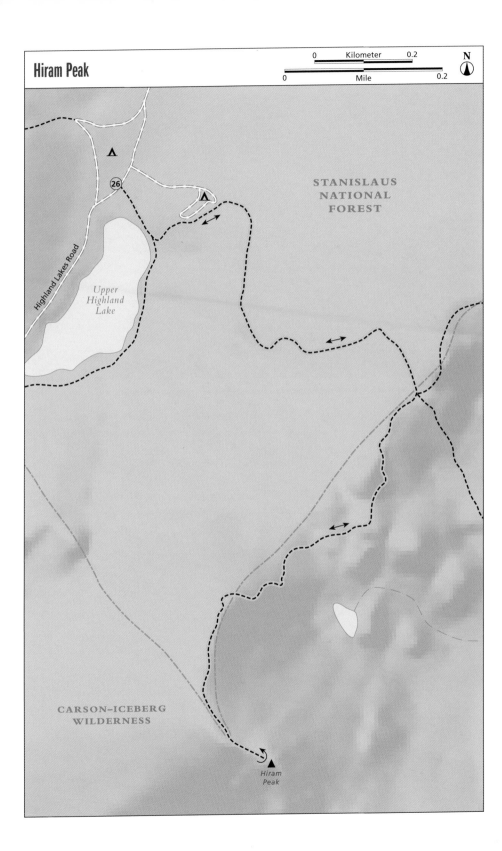

Hiram Peak

0   Kilometer   0.2
0   Mile   0.2

N

STANISLAUS
NATIONAL
FOREST

Highland Lakes Road

26

Upper
Highland
Lake

CARSON–ICEBERG
WILDERNESS

Hiram
Peak

Hiram Peak stands among the tallest mountains of Carson-Iceberg Wilderness.

Pioneer John Ebbetts followed in 1851 and suggested the route for a transcontinental railroad to surveyor George Goddard. After Ebbetts died in a steamboat explosion in 1854, Goddard named the pass after him.

John "Snowshoe" Thompson delivered mail through this area on his cross-country skis from 1856 to 1876.

Our mountain's name honors Hiram Tyre, who grazed cattle in the region.

MORE MOUNTAIN MATTERS

Highland Lakes Road opens later than Ebbetts Pass, so check with the Forest Service if you're considering a trip in the early season. Skiers who arrive soon enough may find sufficient snow on the mountain's north face to allow a few turns.

Though just a stone's throw apart, the two Highland Lakes are headwaters for two different watersheds. The northeastern lake flows into the Mokelumne River drainage; the southwestern one flows into the Stanislaus River drainage.

Highland Lakes offer brook trout fishing and camping.

27 GRANITE CHIEF

Experience a taste of alpine wilderness right beside a popular ski area. Granite Chief delivers a rewarding adventure amid spectacular scenery.

Distance: 10 miles round-trip (all on trails)
Time: 4 to 6 hours
Difficulty: Class 2; moderate
Land agency: Tahoe National Forest
Nearest facilities: Olympic Valley

Trailhead elevation: 6,230 feet
Summit elevation: 9,006 feet
Elevation gain: 2,776 feet
Best season: June–Oct
Permits: None needed

FINDING THE TRAILHEAD

Olympic Valley lies west of Highway 89 between Truckee and Tahoe City. Take the main road past the ski area to Chamonix Place at the village's western edge. Our trail begins north of Olympic Village Inn.

CLIMBING THE MOUNTAIN

Hike west in Shirley Canyon, soon approaching the creek where it cascades over granite boulders. Turn right to climb up a path connecting with Granite Chief Trail. Then turn left onto our route which meanders to the west as it ascends the glacially sculpted valley, passing streams, granite walls, and boulders.

A left turn onto Pacific Crest Trail arrives about two-thirds of the way through the total distance and elevation gain. Our path leads south to a meadow due east of our destination. Climbing steepens as we approach the ski lift station. A use trail ascends the last 400 feet to the peak.

Our summit view boasts dozens of mountain summits in the west Lake Tahoe area, including Jobs Peak, Ellis Peak, and Mount Judah.

MILES AND DIRECTIONS

0.0   From Chamonix Place, hike west

0.4   Turn right (north) toward Granite Chief Trail

0.7   Turn left (west) onto Granite Chief Trail

3.4   Turn left (south) onto Pacific Crest Trail

4.8   At the ski lift station, follow a use trail to the west

5.0   Summit

10.0 Arrive back at the trailhead

HIGH HISTORY: OLYMPIC GLORY, NAME-CHANGING STORY

The Washoe Tribe occupied this valley prior to the Gold Rush. The ski resort that opened in 1949 hosted the Winter Olympics in 1960. Skier Penny Pitou won silver

Granite Chief

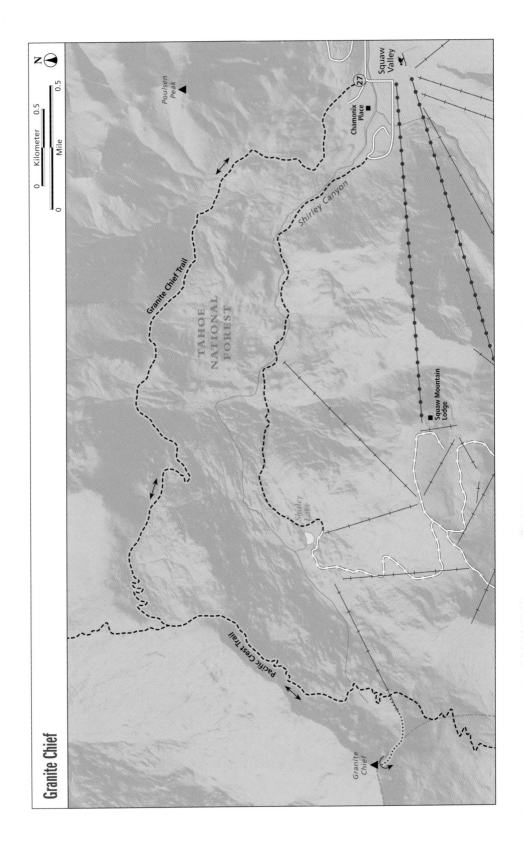

medals in both the downhill and giant slalom races to highlight American results, though the Soviet Union beat the United States in the total medal count, 21–10. The Games led to road improvements and a population boom around Lake Tahoe. Congress passed the California Wilderness Act of 1984, which protected Granite Chief Wilderness within Tahoe National Forest. After the Washoe campaigned for years, the ski resort agreed to remove the racist and sexist slur from its name in 2021.

Shirley Canyon features soothing scenery in the hike's first mile.

28 JOBS PEAK

A steep but short outing leads to one of the highest summits in the Lake Tahoe area. Even during the peak summer season, this mountain sees few hikers. A high-clearance vehicle may be needed to reach the trailhead.

Distance: 4.4 miles round-trip (all on trails)
Time: 3 to 4 hours
Difficulty: Class 1; strenuous (for elevation gain)
Land agency: Humboldt-Toiyabe National Forest

Nearest facilities: South Lake Tahoe
Trailhead elevation: 8,600 feet
Summit elevation: 10,663 feet
Elevation gain: 2,063 feet
Best season: June–Oct
Permits: None needed

FINDING THE TRAILHEAD

From South Lake Tahoe, take Highway 89 southeast. About a mile east of Luther Pass, turn left onto Willow Creek Road (Forest Road 051); at this writing, it has no road sign. The dirt road may be smooth and accessible or it could be rough and muddy; proceed with caution. If conditions permit, drive northeast for about 5 miles to the road's end. Find our trail to the north.

Freel Peak and Jobs Sister could inspire an extended outing.

Jobs Peak

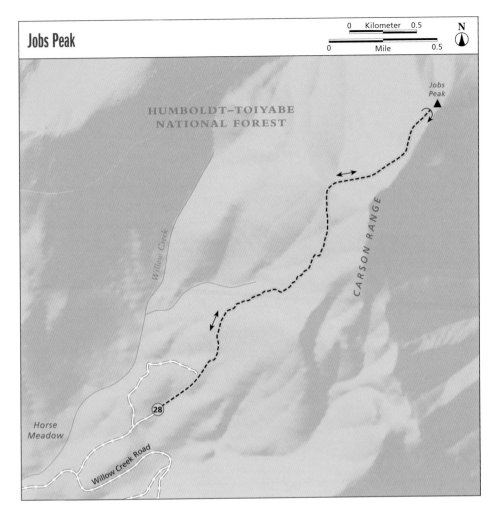

CLIMBING THE MOUNTAIN

Our path leads northeast on an old forest road that soon transitions to a footpath. Climb through a forest of conifers that thankfully shade our ascent. The trail gains about a thousand feet per mile, so take your time.

As we climb, nearby Freel Peak and Jobs Sister come into view. Our main objective waits to reveal itself until we clear a ridge at about 10,200 feet. Then Jobs Peak stands just a half-mile away.

At the summit, look for a mailbox that contains a register. Enjoy the view of Jobs Sister, Freel Peak, Lake Tahoe, and Nevada's Carson Valley.

MORE MOUNTAIN MATTERS
Ambitious hikers combine this outing with ascents of Jobs Sister and Freel Peak to achieve a three-summit day.

MILES AND DIRECTIONS

0.0 From the road's end parking area, hike north

2.2 Summit

4.4 Arrive back at the trailhead

HIGH HISTORY: IMMODEST MOUNTAINEER?

The mountain's name honors Moses Job, a settler who opened a store in nearby Sheridan, Nevada, in the 1850s. Local historians claim that "Moses Job, an irrepressible man, climbed the peak, planted an American flag and with a shout named the peak after himself!" The peak and its two neighbors were once called Job's Group of Mountains. Today the other summits are called Jobs Sister, after his sibling, and Freel Peak, for late-1800s miner and rancher James Freel.

29 STANISLAUS PEAK

Named for a Native American, volcanic Stanislaus Peak boasts an interesting human and geologic history. Despite its unique distinctions, the mountain overlooking Carson-Iceberg Wilderness sees few visitors. If you're traveling Highway 108 over Sonora Pass, it deserves a closer look.

Distance: 8 miles round-trip (on trails, use trails, and cross-country)
Time: 4 to 6 hours
Difficulty: Class 2; strenuous (for distance and elevation)
Land agency: Stanislaus National Forest

Nearest facilities: Kennedy Meadows
Trailhead elevation: 9,432 feet
Summit elevation: 11,233 feet
Elevation gain: 1,801 feet
Best season: June–Oct
Permits: None needed

FINDING THE TRAILHEAD

Park in a dirt lot at St. Marys Pass trailhead, located north of Highway 108 about 0.8 mile west of Sonora Pass. A trailhead sign is visible beside the parking area. There's also a pullout on the south side of the road. Follow the dirt road to the north.

CLIMBING THE MOUNTAIN

Our path starts as a dirt road and soon becomes a single-track trail. Hike steadily up to St. Marys Pass, soon climbing above tree line into a land of scattered pines, sage, and wildflowers.

At the saddle, you'll find a wilderness boundary sign and a four-way junction. Go straight toward the red, round cone standing prominently to the north. The route contours a ridge that leads to the base of our mountain.

This trail ends at the plateau about a half-mile southeast of our goal. From here on, you may find use trails or you may get to plot your own course to gain the last 600 feet up the peak's southeast flank.

Landmarks of our summit view include nearby Sonora and Leavitt Peaks, Hiram and Highland Peaks neighboring Ebbetts Pass, and Round Top and Mount Tallac near Lake Tahoe.

MILES AND DIRECTIONS

0.0 Hike north from trailhead toward St. Marys Pass

1.2 Go straight (north) at St. Marys Pass

4.0 Summit

8.0 Arrive back at the trailhead

HIGH HISTORY: ONE MAN, TWO WORLDS, THREE NAMES

Our mountain's name honors a Yokut originally named Cucunuchi who was born near present-day Modesto in 1798. The Spanish forced him and his family to Mission San Jose in 1821. Friars baptized him with the name Estanislao, after a Polish saint, and he rose to the position of *alcalde*, holding some authority within the mission. But Estanislao and about 400 followers escaped in 1827, likely angry at the padres' treatment of indigenous people.

Stanislaus Peak's summit view impresses visitors, including four-legged ones.

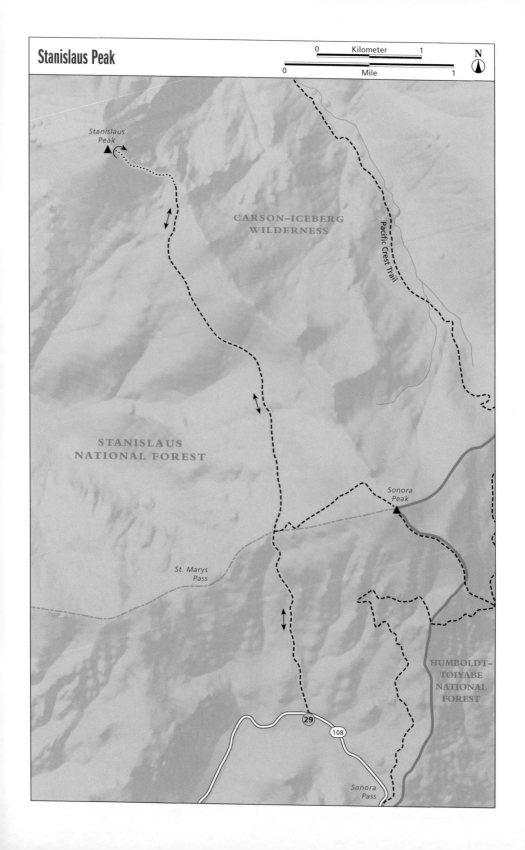

0   Kilometer   1

0   Mile   1

N

Stanislaus
Peak

CARSON–ICEBERG
WILDERNESS

Pacific Crest Trail

STANISLAUS
NATIONAL FOREST

Sonora
Peak

St. Marys
Pass

HUMBOLDT–
TOIYABE
NATIONAL
FOREST

29

108

Sonora
Pass

Estanislao rallied up to 4,000 other Yokuts and Chumash, leading multiple raids on the missions and Mexican settlers over the next two years. After several efforts, the Mexican army subdued his attacks in 1829. Surprisingly, the Mexican governor pardoned Estanislao and his followers. Estanislao returned to Mission San Jose in 1834 and taught the Yokut language until he died in 1838, possibly of smallpox.

Today Stanislaus Peak stands as one of the few California mountains named after a Native American. A river, county, and national forest honor him, too. But ironically the title which they all use is an anglicized version of a Spanish name, not the original Yokut-given name of Cucunuchi.

Mount Tallac

30 MOUNT TALLAC

The most prominent peak in Lake Tahoe Basin provides the best view of the lake and perhaps the best adventure in the area. Despite a thigh-burning climb, it attracts thousands of climbers each year.

Distance: 9.6 miles round-trip (all on trails)
Time: 6 to 8 hours
Difficulty: Class 2; strenuous (for distance and elevation gain)
Land agency: Lake Tahoe Basin Management Unit

Nearest facilities: South Lake Tahoe
Trailhead elevation: 6,480 feet
Summit elevation: 9,735 feet
Elevation gain: 3,255 feet
Best season: June–Oct
Permits: Required

FINDING THE TRAILHEAD

From South Lake Tahoe, take Highway 89 northwest from the Highway 50 junction and drive 3.9 miles toward Emerald Bay. Turn left onto Mount Tallac Road (a forest sign for Camp Concord and Camp Shelly marks the turnoff, which is straight across the highway from Baldwin Beach) and drive about a mile to the parking area and trailhead.

CLIMBING THE MOUNTAIN

Get a self-issued permit at the trailhead to enter Desolation Wilderness. Start the hike through the forest as the trail begins to climb. Fallen Leaf Lake comes into view as you climb up and along a sharp ridge in about half a mile. The wilderness boundary and Floating Island Lake follow within the next mile. Enjoy the shade of the forest's pines, cedars, and oaks while you can because you're about to climb into a realm of rock, sun, and wind. Stay right, as a side trail leads left and steeply down to Fallen Leaf Lake. Continue south to Cathedral Lake; this is the last reliable source of water.

There are four trail junctions between Cathedral Lake and the summit, some offering variations that also lead to the summit, but the simplest approach is to simply turn right at all four going up (and left at all four going down). Our path veers west through Cathedral Basin as we climb above tree line. Here the route becomes steep and leads over a large talus slope. After gaining a ridge, the climbing eases as the path turns north and leads through scattered trees on the mountain's south slope.

As you take the final steps, you will reach a perch overlooking magnificent Lake Tahoe. Hang on to your hat in the wind, find a good sitting rock, and take some time to enjoy the peerless view before descending.

MILES AND DIRECTIONS

- 0.0 From Mount Tallac Road parking lot, hike south on the trail
- 2.4 Stay right (south) at junction with trail to Fallen Leaf Lake
- 3.1 Turn right (north) at trail junction
- 3.8 Turn right (northwest) at trail junction

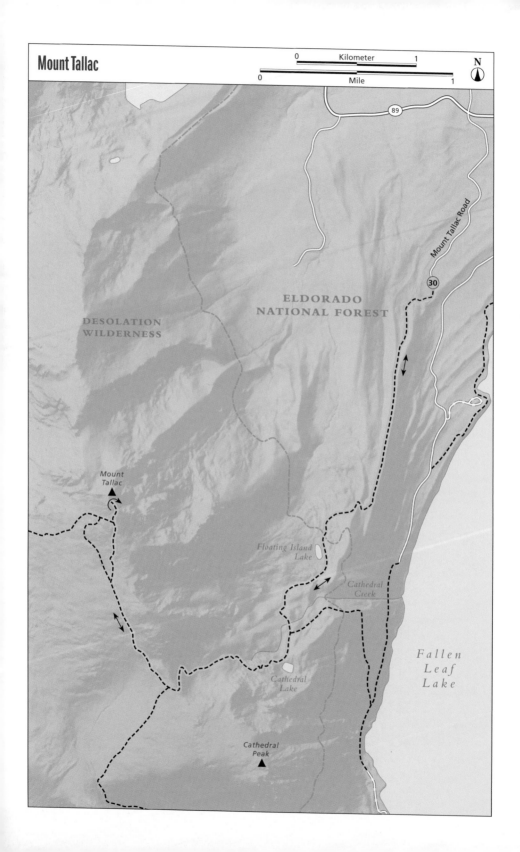

Mount Tallac

0   Kilometer   1

0   Mile   1

N

89

ELDORADO
NATIONAL FOREST

Mount Tallac Road

30

DESOLATION
WILDERNESS

Mount
Tallac

Floating Island
Lake

Cathedral
Creek

Cathedral
Lake

Fallen
Leaf
Lake

Cathedral
Peak

Mount Tallac boasts an inspiring view of Lake Tahoe.

4.3 Turn right (north) at trail junction

4.6 Turn right (north) at trail junction

4.8 Summit

9.6 Arrive back at the trailhead

HIGH HISTORY: BEWARE A MELTED CROSS

The Washoe called the peak *Talah-act*, meaning "Great Mountain." Whitney Survey maps labeled it "Crystal Peak" in the 1860s. Members of the Wheeler Survey led by Lt. Montgomery Macomb made the first documented ascent in 1876 and revived the indigenous name as "Tallac" in 1877. A snow cross appears on the northeast face. Legends predict that when it melts, it forebodes a heavy winter, war, or even the end of the world.

MORE MOUNTAIN MATTERS

Snowfields cover the path in places early in the season, requiring careful footing and route finding. Be careful following the footprints of earlier hikers through snow because they sometimes lead off the trail.

This hike becomes hot, dusty, and crowded in the summer months; consider an early start. Rough, rocky trail on the upper half of this route makes hiking poles especially helpful.

Backcountry skiers most commonly approach from the junction of Highway 89 and Spring Creek Road and ascend the mountain's northeast bowl. This is an experts-only proposition that requires avalanche awareness.

MORE MOUNTAINS IN THE SIERRA NEVADA

G. SIERRA BUTTES

Distance: 4.6 miles round-trip (on dirt roads and trails)
Time: 2 to 4 hours
Difficulty: Class 1; moderate
Land agency: Tahoe National Forest
Nearest facilities: Sierra City
Trailhead elevation: 7,000 feet
Summit elevation: 8,587 feet
Elevation gain: 1,587 feet
Best season: June–Oct
Permits: None needed

Sierra Buttes

This mountain's fire lookout opened in 1915 and forest employees built its heart-pounding stairs in 1964. From Highway 49 about 5 miles east of Sierra City, turn onto Gold Lake Highway. Follow signs to a trailhead and parking area for Sierra Buttes and Pacific Crest Trail. Our hike starts on a southbound dirt road overlapping the PCT. Eventually we turn left to leave the PCT and climb steeply up switchbacks to the glacier-carved summit. Views of the Lake Basin area are worth the bold climb up the 176 stairs, so summon your courage!

H. ELLIS PEAK

Distance: 6.2 miles round-trip (all on trails)
Time: 3 to 4 hours
Difficulty: Class 1; moderate
Land agency: Tahoe National Forest
Nearest facilities: Tahoe Pines
Trailhead elevation: 7,775 feet
Summit elevation: 8,740 feet
Elevation gain: 1,667 feet
Best season: June–Oct
Permits: None needed

Ellis Peak

This mountain and adjacent lake are named for Jack "Jock" Ellis, a former miner who established a ranch nearby in 1863. From Highway 89 about a quarter-mile north of Eagle Rock, turn west onto Barker Pass Road and drive 6.9 miles to Barker Pass, which has roadside parking; this road opens annually on June 15 and closes on November 5. The signed trail to the south leads to the summit, which provides phenomenal views of Lake Tahoe to the east and Desolation Wilderness to the south. A detour to Ellis Lake adds less than a mile round-trip. Part of this route and alternative trails allow bicycles.

I. LOOKOUT PEAK

Distance: 10.4 miles round-trip (all on trails)
Time: 5 to 7 hours
Difficulty: Class 3; strenuous (for distance, elevation gain, and summit scramble)
Land agency: Kings Canyon National Park
Nearest facilities: Cedar Grove
Trailhead elevation: 4,670 feet
Summit elevation: 8,531 feet
Elevation gain: 3,861 feet
Best season: June–Oct
Permits: None needed

Lookout Peak

Elisha Winchell made the first known ascent on September 27, 1868. Park near Cedar Grove and find Don Cecil Trail leading south of the highway about 200 yards east of the intersection with North Side Drive. A strenuous but straightforward hike leads to the summit area. To reach the actual summit requires a Class 3 scramble. A view of Kings Canyon, Sequoia National Forest, Monarch Wilderness, and distant High Sierra peaks rewards the effort.

Death Valley and Eastern Sierra Nevada

Marie Lake

EASTSIDE

Bob Coomber's five years of preparation came down to the final feet on August 24, 2007. The wheelchair climber known as 4 Wheel Bob muscled his way up White Mountain for 8 miles. Then the jeep road he followed got even steeper beneath the 14,246-foot summit.

"The final twenty feet were the toughest. It took all I had left," Coomber recalled. "I was almost in tears. Only exhaustion kept me from completely breaking down."

At age 20, Coomber contracted diabetes that led to osteoporosis, confining him to a wheelchair. But at 52, he became the first (and still only) wheelchair climber to summit a California "14er" (a mountain peak with an elevation of at least 14,000 feet).

"4 Wheel Bob hits the summit!" he wrote in the summit register. "It's my wish that others follow, even if the trail is gnarly."

California's Eastern Sierra and high desert mountains, known as the Eastside, deliver abundant challenges and rewards.

Eastern Sierra mountains, the result of subduction between tectonic plates, include thirteen of California's fifteen summits exceeding 14,000 feet. They stand over Owens Valley to their east and block eastbound precipitation. This contributes to the dry conditions of the White and Inyo mountain ranges, the upper Mojave Desert, and Death Valley, the hottest place on Earth.

The region falls within Inyo and Mono Counties, which rank among the state's smallest by population (32,000 people combined) and largest by area, covering 14,000 square miles.

To much of California, this is remote territory, especially in winter. Highways 4, 108, and 120 normally open in May or June and close with the first major snows of fall or winter. Highway 395 provides year-round access from the north and south.

Altitude acclimatization is essential, as several trailheads exceed 9,000 feet. Climbers should take a few days to adjust before attempting difficult outings.

Speaking of difficult, Coomber set his sights on an even greater challenge after White Mountain: trekking 24 miles over formidable Kearsarge Pass. He's made three attempts since 2013. A rockfall blocked his last effort. Then the need for a kidney transplant sidelined him.

Still, 4 Wheel Bob hasn't ruled out another try.

"I'd love to head over there again," he said.

His motto?

"No more excuses."

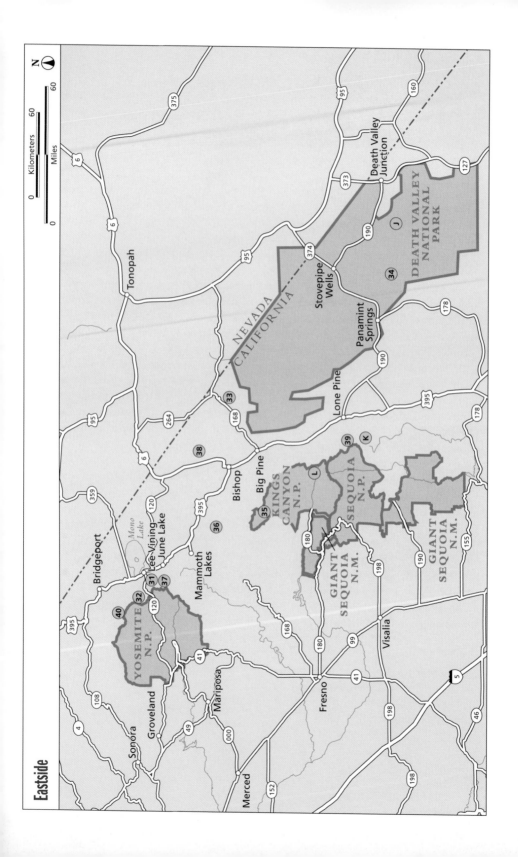

Eastside

Eastside Peaks at a Glance

SUMMIT	DISTANCE	DIFFICULTY	LAND AGENCY	SUMMIT ELEVATION	ELEVATION GAIN	BEST SEASON
31. Reversed Peak	6 miles	Class 2; easy to moderate	Inyo National Forest	9,459 feet	1,782 feet	June–Oct
32. Tioga Peak	3 miles	Class 1; moderate	Inyo National Forest	11,526 feet	1,783 feet	June–Oct
33. Chocolate Mountain	5.4 miles	Class 1; moderate	Bureau of Land Management	7,703 feet	1,432 feet	year round
34. Wildrose Peak	8.4 miles	Class 1; moderate	Death Valley National Park	9,064 feet	2,158 feet	April–Nov
35. Mount Solomons	1.5 miles	Class 2; moderate to strenuous	Kings Canyon National Park	13,034 feet	1,079 feet	July–Sept
36. Mount Starr	7.8 miles	Class 2; moderate to strenuous	Inyo National Forest	12,835 feet	2,705 feet	June–Oct
37. Carson Peak	10.6 miles	Class 2; strenuous	Inyo National Forest	10,912 feet	3,669 feet	June–Oct
38. White Mountain	15 miles	Class 1; strenuous	Inyo National Forest	14,252 feet	2,552 feet	June–Oct
39. Lone Pine Peak	10.4 miles	Class 2; strenuous	Inyo National Forest	12,949 feet	4,900 feet	June–Oct
40. Matterhorn Peak	12 miles	Class 3; strenuous	Humboldt-Toiyabe National Forest	12,279 feet	5,187	June–Oct
J. Dante Peak	0.8 mile	Class 1; easy	Death Valley National Park	5,704 feet	250 feet	year-round
K. Trail Peak	6.4 miles	Class 2; moderate	Inyo National Forest	11,617 feet	1,667 feet	June–Oct
L. Mount Gould	10.2 miles	Class 3; strenuous	Inyo National Forest	13,005 feet	3,805 feet	June–Oct

31 REVERSED PEAK

A pleasant hike provides a scenic outing in the heart of the June Lake area. The best starter mountain among our Eastside summits delivers a good warm-up and altitude acclimatization for the more-challenging climbs of the high desert and eastern Sierra.

Distance: 6 miles on a loop (all on trails)
Time: 3 to 4 hours
Difficulty: Class 2; easy to moderate
Land agency: Inyo National Forest
Nearest facilities: June Lake

Trailhead elevation: 7,677 feet
Summit elevation: 9,459 feet
Elevation gain: 1,782 feet
Best season: June–Oct
Permits: None required

FINDING THE TRAILHEAD

From June Lake Junction on Highway 395 (10 miles south of Lee Vining), drive southwest on Highway 158 for about 3.75 miles to Northshore Drive. Turn right, drive another 0.4 mile to a dirt pullout on the west side of the road, and park.

CLIMBING THE MOUNTAIN

Hike on the dirt road that leads to a single-track trail. Here the climbing begins as the path curves around a ridge in a clockwise semicircle.

Continue northeast past a pond and scattered pines. Aspens also grow here and reward fall hikers with a golden glow. Reach a signed trail junction after about 2 miles; turn left and ascend a second ridge to the north. Terrain flattens briefly and then a final climb takes us to granite boulders that cap the summit. To top the highest one will take a few minutes of Class 2 scrambling.

Our summit vantage point features a 360-degree view of the June Lake area, including Carson Peak to the south, Kuna Peak and Mount Lewis to the west, Grant Lake and Mono Lake to the north, and many other features of Inyo National Forest and Ansel Adams Wilderness.

When you descend, return to the signed trail junction and turn left to complete Reversed Trail Loop. This variation descends more directly toward Northshore Drive and then follows beside it until you reach your starting point again.

MILES AND DIRECTIONS

0.0   Hike west on a dirt road that soon becomes a trail, climbing and curving northeast

1.9   Turn left (north) at trail junction

3.2   Summit

4.5   After descending the summit spur trail to the trail junction, turn left (east)

5.0   Turn right (south) where trail meets dirt road

5.2   Take southbound trail beside Northshore Drive

6.0   Arrive back at the trailhead

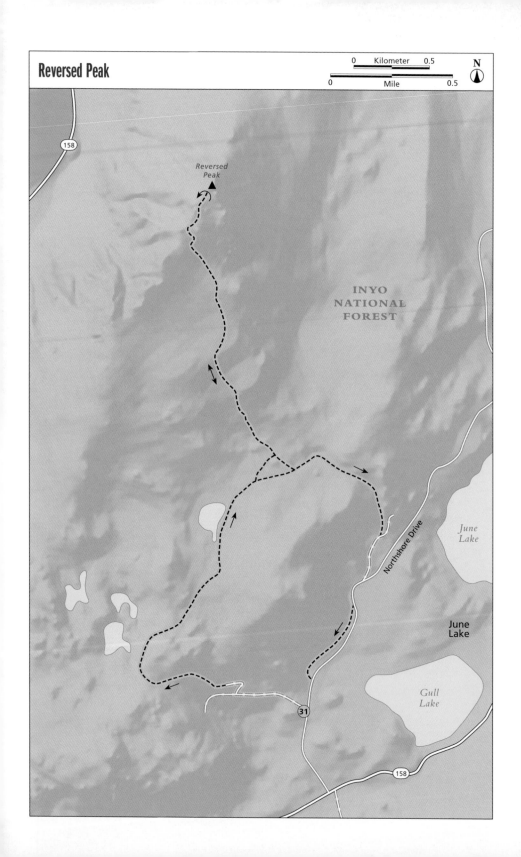

Reversed Peak

Reversed
Peak

0   Kilometer   0.5

0   Mile   0.5

N

158

INYO
NATIONAL
FOREST

Northshore Drive

June
Lake

June
Lake

Gull
Lake

31

158

Kuna Peak and Mount Lewis stand east of the Reversed Peak summit.

HIGH HISTORY: "REVERSED" DRAINAGE INSPIRED NAME

Geologists believe that Reversed Peak split the Rush Creek Glacier that formed June Lake's horseshoe-shaped valley. USGS surveyors exploring this area reported that "the ancient drainage has been reversed by the deposition of morainal debris; we have therefore called the stream draining June and Gull lakes Reversed Creek." Surveyors also named the peak after the creek, and the titles appeared on maps by 1901.

MORE MOUNTAIN MATTERS

The town of June Lake sprouted in the 1920s as a popular stop for Southern Californians who drove to Yosemite up the new El Camino Sierra, the road now known as Highway 395.

Tioga Peak

32 TIOGA PEAK

A short outing delivers a High Sierra feeling on this Hoover Wilderness mountain just outside Yosemite. In terms of effort and payoff, Tioga Peak rates among the best outings in the state.

Distance: 3 miles round-trip (on trails and use trails)	**Trailhead elevation:** 9,743 feet
Time: 2 to 3 hours	**Summit elevation:** 11,526 feet
Difficulty: Class 1; moderate	**Elevation gain:** 1,783 feet
Land agency: Inyo National Forest	**Best season:** June–Oct
Nearest facilities: Lee Vining	**Permits:** None needed

FINDING THE TRAILHEAD

 From Highway 120 between Tioga Lake and Ellery Lake (2 miles outside Yosemite's Tioga Pass entrance), turn northwest onto Saddlebag Lake Road and drive 1.2 miles to a trailhead parking area. The road alternates between pavement and dirt and generally does not require a high-clearance vehicle. Find Gardisky Lake Trail to the north.

CLIMBING THE MOUNTAIN

Before beginning, look east to see Tioga Peak. Once on your way up Gardisky Lake Trail, white pines, lodgepole pines, and mountain hemlocks will obscure our destination from view for a while. Steep but short, our path crosses a stream a few times as it winds its way up the hillside.

Once you reach a plateau and Gardisky Lake comes into view, turn right (southeast) off the main trail and follow a use trail toward Tioga Peak. Faint at first, the path becomes clearer as you near the mountain and leads straight to its top.

Mount Conness, Lee Vining Peak, and Mount Dana stand out in our spectacular summit view, which also affords a rewarding look at the Yosemite high country.

MILES AND DIRECTIONS

- 0.0   Hike northeast on Gardisky Lake Trail
- 0.7   Turn right (southeast) off the main trail onto a use trail
- 1.5   Summit
- 3.0   Arrive back at the trailhead

MORE MOUNTAIN MATTERS

Nearby Gardisky Lake deserves a short detour on your way up or down the mountain. Anglers speak highly of it. Miner Albert Gardisky inspired the lake's name. After arriving around 1914, he built the lodge, store, and cabins that became nearby Tioga Pass Resort.

Tioga Peak

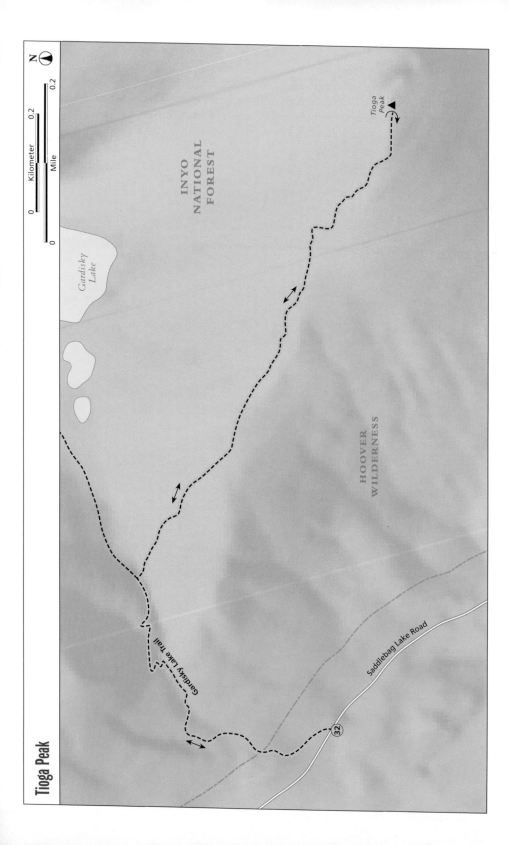

Tioga Peak looks upon Mount Dana and Yosemite's high summits.

HIGH HISTORY: MINERS MISS, BUT BUILD BEAUTIFUL BYWAY

Miner Lee Vining founded a nearby camp in 1852 that grew into the town that's now named for him. His name is also attached to geologic features and events that happened quite a bit earlier: Lee Vining Glacier carved the steep Lee Vining Canyon and exposed Tioga Peak's metamorphic rock.

Tioga Peak takes its name from the nearby Tioga Mine, which took its name from New York's Tioga River, which took its name from the Mohawk and Iroquois term *tioga*, which means "where it forks."

In the 1880s mining interests also built Tioga Road, which climbs steeply up Lee Vining Canyon. When the mines failed to prosper, the road fell into disuse until 1915, when generous benefactors bought out the owners and sold it to Yosemite for $10. A marvel of engineering made the breathtaking highway usable for automobiles, opening access to the park from the east.

33 CHOCOLATE MOUNTAIN

Sweet as its name, Chocolate Mountain stands over a seldom-visited desert preserve near the state's eastern border. A moderate ascent affords views of three mountain ranges in a corner of California that few ever see.

Distance: 5.4 miles round-trip (all on trails)
Time: 3 to 4 hours
Difficulty: Class 1; moderate
Land agency: Bureau of Land Management

Nearest facilities: Big Pine
Trailhead elevation: 6,271 feet
Summit elevation: 7,703 feet
Elevation gain: 1,432 feet
Best season: Year-round
Permits: None needed

FINDING THE TRAILHEAD

From Big Pine, take Highway 168 northeast for 33 miles. At Gilbert Pass, turn right (south) onto a dirt road and drive past a Piper Mountain Wilderness sign for 0.3 mile to a small parking area. The trail leads to the southwest.

CLIMBING THE MOUNTAIN

This path was once a four-wheel-drive route that closed to automobiles after becoming a wilderness area. Vegetation partially obscures the old dirt road, but it's still clear enough to follow fairly easily.

Our trail leads southwest and quickly turns west and south, curving around a hill. We then climb through a slot between two other modest summits. The route turns sharply east as our destination comes into view about a mile away. Pinyon pines, desert wildflowers, and a few cacti line the path.

Chocolate Mountain, consisting of granite and dark basaltic lava, looks much like a giant chocolate sundae dropped in the desert. However, with green sage scattered across much of its surface, it could just as well be called Mint Chocolate Mountain. Keep an eye out for a sharp right turn leading up the northwest face to its peak, where a large juniper tree stands, and you'll find a register that's rarely signed.

From the top we can see White Mountain, Death Valley, the Piper, Sylvania, and Inyo mountain ranges, and distant Sierra peaks like Mount Whitney and Mount Langley.

If you treat yourself to a chocolate ice cream after descending, you will have earned it more than most people back in town.

MORE MOUNTAIN MATTERS

Keep an eye out for desert bighorn sheep that occupy at least three areas within the wilderness. Piper Mountain Wilderness also boasts the state's northernmost Joshua trees.

Winter visitors may need cross-country skis or snowshoes.

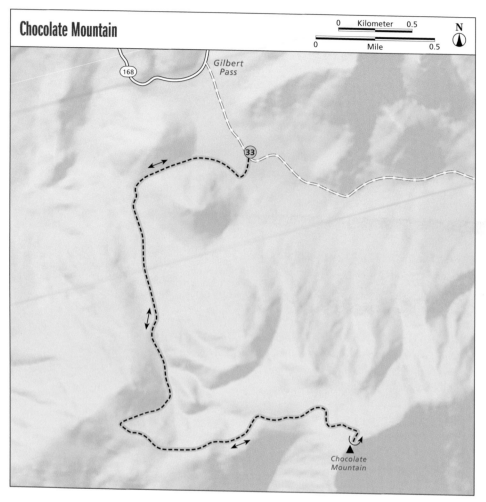

MILES AND DIRECTIONS

0.0 Hike southwest from trailhead

2.2 Turn right (south) onto summit spur trail

2.7 Summit

5.4 Arrive back at the trailhead

HIGH HISTORY: DESERT DEFENDERS DELIVER DECREE

Piper Mountain Wilderness gained federal protection under the 1994 California Desert Protection Act. The law sponsored by California senator Dianne Feinstein and signed by President Bill Clinton preserved more than 9 million acres, establishing Death Valley National Park, Joshua Tree National Park, and Mojave National Preserve. Piper Mountain Wilderness encompasses 72,000 acres, including parts of the Piper, Sylvania, and Inyo mountain ranges.

Chocolate Mountain shows visitors a vast portion of Death Valley National Park.

Highway 168 was originally part of the coast-to-coast Roosevelt Midland Trail, established in 1913 as one of the nation's first interstate routes.

Wildrose Peak

34 WILDROSE PEAK

A moderate hike climbs to an inspiring viewpoint above the desert and delivers temperatures far cooler than the surrounding and scorching lowlands. Long enough to challenge but short enough to enjoy, Wildrose Peak makes a perfect introduction to Death Valley National Park.

Distance: 8.4 miles round-trip (all on trails)
Time: 5 to 6 hours
Difficulty: Class 1; moderate
Land agency: Death Valley National Park

Nearest facilities: Panamint Springs
Trailhead elevation: 6,906 feet
Summit elevation: 9,064 feet
Elevation gain: 2,158 feet
Best season: April–Nov
Permits: None needed

FINDING THE TRAILHEAD

From Highway 190, take either Panamint Valley Road or Emigrant Canyon Road south to Wildrose Canyon Road / Charcoal Kiln Road. Drive east for about 7 miles past Wildrose Campground to the charcoal kilns and park south of the road. The paved road transitions to dirt and gravel for the last few miles, which is generally passable for low-clearance vehicles. Park south of the road. Our trail begins to the north beside the kilns.

CLIMBING THE MOUNTAIN

Our journey begins through a forest of pinyon pine and juniper trees. The northbound path gradually contours up hillsides curving east. After about 1.8 miles and some 800 feet of elevation gain, the trail crests a saddle allowing the first broad view of the park's namesake valley to the east. As our route turns west, the path leads up the mountain's east ridge and the peak comes into view. Switchbacks climb up the final mile.

Remarkably, the summit offers a view of both Badwater Basin to the east and Mount Whitney to the west, the lowest and highest points of the continent both visible from the same point. In addition, the taller and tougher Telescope Peak to the south will give you something to think about on your descent.

MILES AND DIRECTIONS

0.0   Hike north from the trailhead

1.8   Saddle

4.2   Summit

8.4   Arrive back at the trailhead

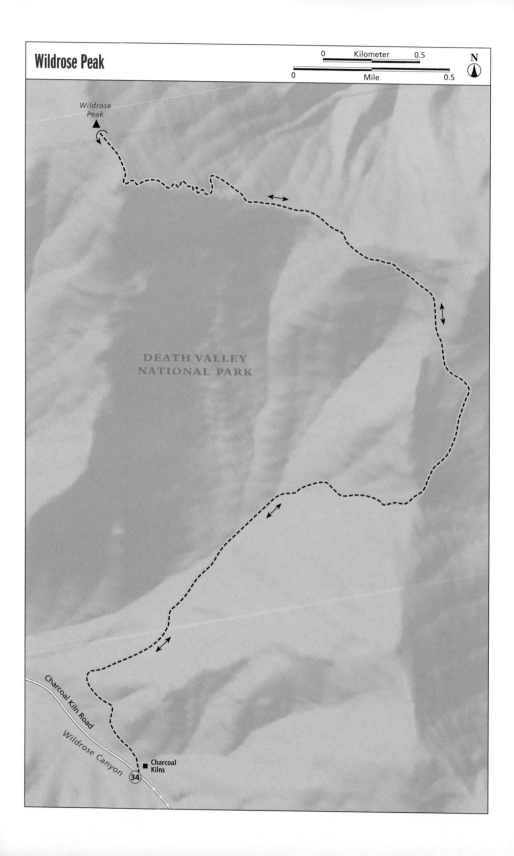

Wildrose Peak

0   Kilometer   0.5
0   Mile   0.5

N

Wildrose
Peak

DEATH VALLEY
NATIONAL PARK

Charcoal Kiln Road

Wildrose Canyon

34

■ Charcoal
   Kilns

HIGH HISTORY: TORRID TEMPERATURES, TIMBISHA'S TRIUMPH

Limestone and sandstone in the Panamint Range indicate that this area was once a warm, shallow sea. Plate movement pushed the mountains upward over time and erosion helped shape the peaks visible today.

The Timbisha Shoshone people occupied the area long before others arrived. They called the valley *Tümpisa*, which means "rock paint," in reference to a red clay found there.

Would-be gold miners encountered the Panamint Range in 1849. Exhausted, starving, dehydrated, and lost, the group sent two men for help. Amazingly, the pair trekked nearly 500 wilderness miles and returned with provisions, saving all but one pioneer. As the party left, one of them looked back and said "Good-bye, Death Valley," inspiring the desert's name.

Early accounts described the valley as a "waterless waste" that was "thickly strewn with dead" and with "temperatures that never fell below 130 degrees." While all these claims wildly exaggerated reality, there's no disputing the desert's intense heat. Death Valley holds world records for the hottest air temperature (134 degrees in 1913) and surface temperature (201 degrees in 1972) ever recorded. Nonetheless, it still attracted miners who extracted gold, silver, and borax from the land.

Wildrose Peak delivers a look at the desert's fascinating geology.

Dantes View affords one of the most dramatic outlooks in Death Valley National Park.

Dr. S. G. George and his party named Wildrose Canyon in 1860. Today the name also applies to our mountain to its north and a nearby spring, as well as the charcoal kilns that stand beside our trailhead. Miners built these in 1877 to provide fuel for silver and lead smelters to the west. Tree stumps remaining along our trail show their efforts to fuel the kilns.

Conservationists petitioned to protect Death Valley in the early twentieth century. "How can rocks and sand and silence make us afraid and yet be so wonderful?" asked author Edna Perkins in 1922. President Herbert Hoover established Death Valley National Monument in 1933. Congress made it a national park in 1994.

After decades of effort, the Timbisha Shoshone became the first Native Americans to secure land rights within a national park in 2000. "We never gave up," said Pauline Esteves. "The Timbisha people are part of our homeland, and it is part of us."

MORE MOUNTAIN MATTERS

Charcoal Kiln Road closes to automobiles when snowed over, normally from December through mid-April. Check ahead if considering a winter visit. The same road accesses Telescope Peak, the park's highest point at 11,043 feet, which requires more climbing, hiking, and high-clearance driving.

Filmmakers have produced dozens of films in Death Valley, including the original *Star Wars* in 1976.

35 MOUNT SOLOMONS

As the only backcountry peak of this collection, Mount Solomons breaks our usual mold of single-day summits. But for those hiking the John Muir Trail, it's just a short detour from Muir Pass and perhaps the best summit opportunity (besides Mount Whitney) on the 221-mile journey.

Distance: 1.5 miles round-trip (all cross-country)
Time: 2 hours
Difficulty: Class 2; moderate to strenuous (for elevation and terrain)
Land agency: Kings Canyon National Park

Nearest facilities: If you have to ask, you're in trouble, but probably Muir Trail Ranch, 17 miles to the north
Trailhead elevation: 11,955 feet
Summit elevation: 13,034 feet
Elevation gain: 1,079 feet
Best season: July–Sept
Permits: Required for overnight travel

FINDING THE TRAILHEAD

Hike the John Muir Trail to 11,955-foot Muir Pass in Kings Canyon National Park, 6 miles south of Elevation Lake or 7 miles north of LeConte Ranger Station. Those not hiking the entire Muir can reach Muir Pass from Florence Lake in Sierra National Forest to the west (28 miles) or South Lake in Inyo National Forest to the east (19 miles).

CLIMBING THE MOUNTAIN

This outing beckons John Muir Trail hikers who crave a bonus adventure. In the right conditions, Mount Solomons provides a fun detour and a manageable climb for a "13er," or a mountain with at least 13,000 feet of elevation.

From Muir Pass, follow a use trail or plot your own course up the mountain's north face, curving to your right (west) to avoid the steepest terrain. You will have to scramble over some loose rocks; choose your steps carefully and use poles if you have them.

Our summit on the Goddard Divide stands in the heart of the High Sierra, viewing 14ers such as North Palisade and Split Mountain, dozens of 13ers, and Evolution Basin.

MILES AND DIRECTIONS

0.0   From Muir Pass, climb south to southwest

0.75 Summit

1.5   Arrive back at Muir Pass

HIGH HISTORY: NATIVES' NETWORK, PRICELESS PATH, HISTORIC HUT

Long before the John Muir Trail became a world-renowned backpacking route, Native Americans including the Paiute regularly traveled a network of High Sierra paths they called *Niiümü Poyo*, or "The People's Road."

Mount Solomons

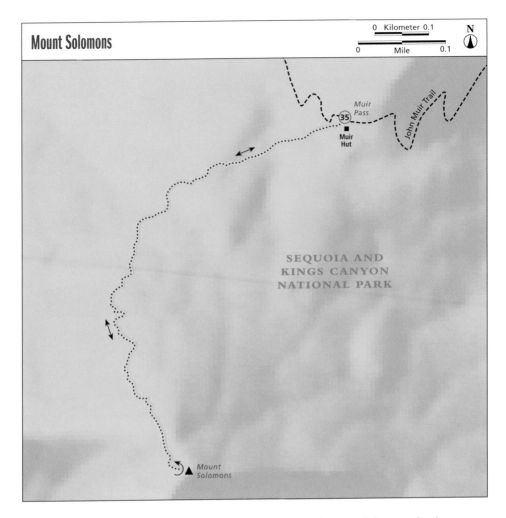

Mount Solomons

Muir
Pass

35

Muir
Hut

John Muir Trail

SEQUOIA AND
KINGS CANYON
NATIONAL PARK

0   Kilometer 0.1

0   Mile   0.1

N

Mount
Solomons

Sierra Club member Theodore Solomons (1870–1947) mapped the area that became Kings Canyon National Park in the 1890s. He proposed a publicly constructed path between Yosemite and Mount Whitney. California committed $10,000 toward the project in 1915. After twenty-three years and several more appropriations, laborers in 1938

MORE MOUNTAIN MATTERS

Start this one early to avoid afternoon thundershowers; you don't want to stand atop a granite 13er if lightning strikes.

Early-season visitors may find the north face snowed over, especially after a big winter, necessitating crampons or microspikes for a safe ascent. If you don't have them, play it smart and skip the climb. Remember, you're a long way from help.

Most backpackers shed their overnight gear at Muir Pass to make an unencumbered ascent.

John Muir Memorial Shelter at Muir Pass has stood since 1931.

finished the trail named (Native Americans would say renamed) after conservationist John Muir.

At roughly the John Muir Trail's midpoint and the beginning of our hike, hikers find two more tributes to the Scottish-born naturalist. Muir Pass carries his name, as does John Muir Memorial Shelter, which the Sierra Club dedicated to its first president in 1931.

But the mountain standing most directly above Muir Pass and the shelter carries the name of Solomons, who explored the region and suggested a trail through it some three decades earlier. M. H. Pramme and F. F. Harms made the first documented ascent on August 12, 1929.

36 MOUNT STARR

Discover the marvelously scenic Rock Creek area on this loop hike in the heart of John Muir Wilderness. A half-day ascent leads beside and above pristine lakes and atop an impressive mountain surrounded by other picturesque summits.

Distance: 7.8 miles round-trip (on trails and cross-country)
Time: 3 to 5 hours
Difficulty: Class 2; moderate to strenuous
Land agency: Inyo National Forest

Nearest facilities: Toms Place
Trailhead elevation: 10,130 feet
Summit elevation: 12,835 feet
Elevation gain: 2,705 feet
Best season: June–Oct
Permits: None needed

FINDING THE TRAILHEAD

From Toms Place on Highway 395, drive southwest on Rock Creek Road for 11 miles until the road ends at Mosquito Flat Trailhead in Little Lakes Valley.

CLIMBING THE MOUNTAIN

Mount Starr and its long summit ridge stand right above the parking area to the southwest. Our trail leads south and right along its base as we start to gain elevation right away. Mack Lake is the first point of interest. Here we find a trail junction; take the right fork toward Mono Pass. As you climb, you may be tempted to ascend the mountain's eastern slope on use trails or cross-country. This does make for a shorter but steeper ascent that's more taxing and less pleasant than the western slope.

Soon we climb above tree line and ascend sandy switchbacks. The next trail junction leads to pretty Ruby Lake, which is worth a quarter-mile detour to the left, but for a direct ascent, stay right for Mono Pass. Terrain steepens here and snow may fill this gully even in summer, especially after a big winter.

Once over the pass, you'll see Mount Starr's western slope on your right. Look for a use trail leading to the summit ridge or, if snow still covers the peak, pick your own line. The long summit ridge has multiple high points; the true summit stands near the middle.

Our view of Inyo National Forest includes Wheeler Ridge and Little Lakes Valley to the east and four 13ers to the south: Mount Mills, Mount Abbot, Mount Dade, and Mount Morgan.

To descend, you could simply reverse your steps as usual. This would make for a 7.8-mile outing. Another option is to go down the eastern slope and rejoin the trail above Mack Lake, making a loop trip. This terrain is steeper and might not be suitable for beginners or children. But for those comfortable going off-trail, it does add variety and cuts about 2 miles from the return trip.

Most Eastern Sierra visitors speed up and down Highway 395 between Mammoth Lakes and Bishop without ever turning onto side roads like this one. If you're one of them, come take a look; one visit will make you wish you'd come sooner.

Mount Starr

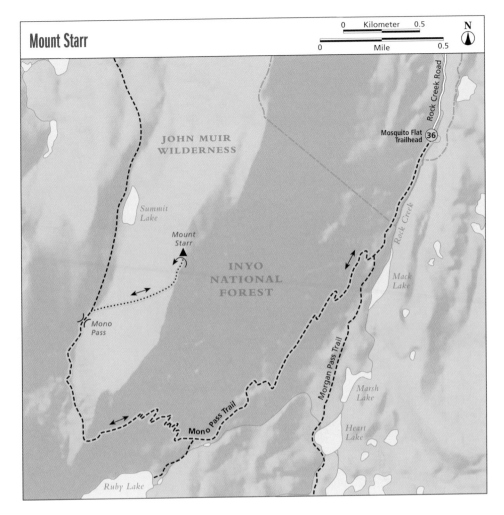

Mount Starr

JOHN MUIR WILDERNESS

Summit Lake

Mount Starr

INYO NATIONAL FOREST

Mono Pass

Mono Pass Trail

Ruby Lake

Mosquito Flat Trailhead 36

Rock Creek Road

Rock Creek

Mack Lake

Morgan Pass Trail

Marsh Lake

Heart Lake

MILES AND DIRECTIONS

0.0 Start at Mosquito Flat Trailhead and hike southwest

0.5 Stay right (southwest) at Mack Lake and Morgan Pass / Mono Pass trail junction

1.9 Turn right (west) at Ruby Lake / Mono Pass trail junction and climb up switchbacks as the path turns north

3.2 At Mono Pass, leave the main trail and take a use trail to the right (northeast) toward the summit

3.9 Summit

7.8 Arrive back at the trailhead

John Muir Wilderness contains multiple peaks exceeding 13,000 feet.

HIGH HISTORY: NAME HONORS A "STARR" MOUNTAINEER

Walter Starr Sr. and Allen Chickering were making the first recorded ascent on July 16, 1896, when a thunderstorm alarmed the pair. "Suddenly everything began to buzz . . . The camera tripod, our fingertips, and even our hair, which stood out straight, seemed to exude electricity. We were badly frightened, and got off the peak as rapidly as possible," they wrote. They named the mountain Electric Peak. But the Sierra Club later renamed the summit in honor of Walter Starr Jr. (1903–1933), a mountaineer, guidebook author, and lawyer who died while climbing in the Minarets.

MORE MOUNTAIN MATTERS

With a trailhead above 10,000 feet, this mountain especially calls for lowlanders to acclimatize before attempting it.

On the way in or out, enjoy Rock Creek Lake, which has a campground. There are ten other campgrounds along Rock Creek Road between Toms Place and Mosquito Flat Trailhead.

37 CARSON PEAK

Challenging but rewarding, Carson Peak takes hikers on a scenic journey through Ansel Adams Wilderness. The ascent requires about 2.6 miles of cross-country travel, though this segment is fairly straightforward for those comfortable with off-trail route finding.

Distance: 10.6 miles round-trip (on trails and cross-country)
Time: 6 to 8 hours
Difficulty: Class 2; strenuous (for distance and elevation gain)
Land agency: Inyo National Forest

Nearest facilities: June Lake
Trailhead elevation: 7,243 feet
Summit elevation: 10,912 feet
Elevation gain: 3,669 feet
Best season: June–Oct
Permits: None needed

FINDING THE TRAILHEAD

From Highway 395, take June Lake Loop Road / Highway 158 to Silver Lake. Park at Rush Creek trailhead and parking area, which is west of the road and north of Silver Lake Resort. Rush Creek Trail begins to the west.

CLIMBING THE MOUNTAIN

Hike south on Rush Creek Trail as it passes Silver Lake Resort and starts gradually climbing. Carson Peak's striking north face stands squarely in view. Our path crosses amazingly steep trolley tracks, which supply the utility buildings above. After a few switchbacks, the trail reaches a junction; turn left to cross Rush Creek and hike east of Agnew Lake. As the ascent steepens, we gain a view of Gem Lake and enter Ansel Adams Wilderness.

There are several stream crossings at Spooky Meadow, which is lush and vibrant and not at all spooky. To the left, Carson's western slope appears steep and daunting, but don't worry—we're taking a friendlier approach.

Watch out for a sharp right turn toward Clark Lakes. When you reach it, leave the trail and hike cross-country to the south. In the middle of the steep ridge facing us, a moderate ramp leads to Carson's summit plateau. Climb the ramp, curve to the left, and follow the plateau to the top.

From the summit, feast your eyes on a truly sensational panorama, which includes Thousand Island Lake, the Ritter Range, the Minarets, San Joaquin Mountain, Reversed Peak, and Mono Lake.

MORE MOUNTAIN MATTERS

Some hikers ascend Carson Peak via Fern Lake. Shorter but steeper, this 8-mile variation also involves off-trail route finding and Class 2 terrain.
The mountain also sees winter ascents by skiers and snowshoers.

Carson Peak

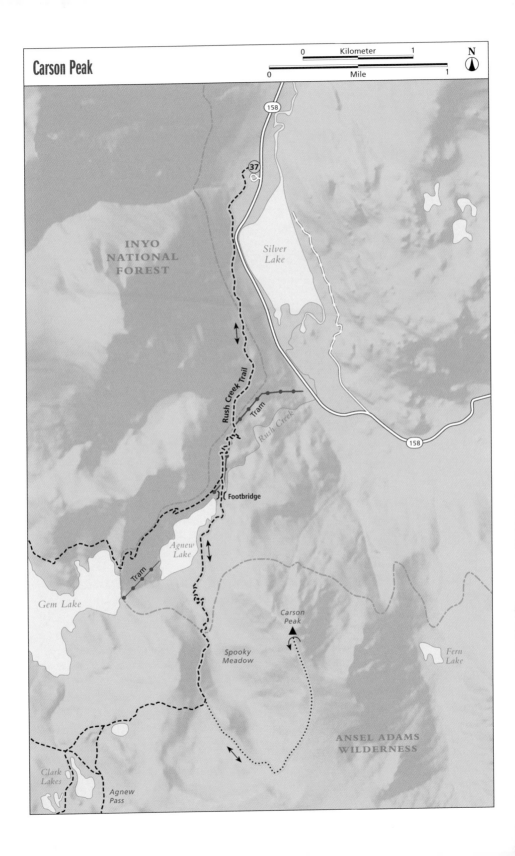

Carson Peak

0   Kilometer   1

0   Mile   1

N

158

37

Silver Lake

INYO NATIONAL FOREST

Rush Creek Trail

Tram

Rush Creek

158

Footbridge

Agnew Lake

Tram

Gem Lake

Carson Peak

Fern Lake

Spooky Meadow

ANSEL ADAMS WILDERNESS

Clark Lakes

Agnew Pass

Carson Peak overlooks Gem Lake and Ansel Adams Wilderness.

MILES AND DIRECTIONS

0.0 Hike south on Rush Creek Trail

2.2 Turn left (south) at trail junction

4.0 Go straight (south), leaving the trail, and ascend the ridge

4.5 Turn left (north) on plateau toward summit

5.3 Summit

10.6 Arrive back at the trailhead

HIGH HISTORY: FISHING, BARS, HOLLYWOOD STARS

This mountain's name honors not the well-known frontiersman Kit Carson but rather Roy Carson, who opened Carson's Camp near Silver Lake in 1916. Carson was a carpenter for the Rush Creek Hydroelectric Project. His "Pasadena fishing buddies" encouraged him to build a resort that became the first commercial attraction of June Lake Loop. His wife Nancy joined as cook and housekeeper in 1919. The camp survives today as Silver Lake Resort, which still uses some of Carson's original buildings.

Lodges, restaurants, and bars in the area multiplied, including the landmark Tiger Bar, which opened in 1932 and still operates today. Hollywood celebrities such as Clark Gable, Charlie Chaplin, and Betty Grable frequented the area. Downhill skiing arrived in the 1940s. June Lake Loop remains a popular stop between Southern California and Yosemite.

38 **WHITE MOUNTAIN**

A dirt road leads to the highest summit of the White Mountain Range, making this the easiest 14er in California. The peak boasts an awesome view of the Sierra Nevada, Death Valley, and the Great Basin, though climbers should not underestimate this long and dry hike at high elevation.

Distance: 15 miles round-trip (all on a dirt road)
Time: 8 to 10 hours
Difficulty: Class 1; strenuous (for distance and elevation)
Land agency: Inyo National Forest

Nearest facilities: Bishop
Trailhead elevation: 11,700 feet
Summit elevation: 14,252 feet
Elevation gain: 2,552 feet
Best season: July–Oct
Permits: None needed

FINDING THE TRAILHEAD

From the town of Big Pine, take Highway 168 east toward the White Mountains for 13 miles. Near Westgard Pass, turn left (north) onto White Mountain Road and drive 26 miles (passing Schulman Grove and Patriarch Grove). The first 10 miles of White Mountain Road / Forest Road 4S01 are paved and the remaining 16.5 miles are on a dirt road, rocky but generally passable for low-clearance vehicles. Park at the locked Barcroft Gate.

PLANNING AND PREPARATION

White Mountain Road is normally clear of snow between late June and November. It's a good idea to check the road status with Inyo National Forest before driving up there.

Water, food, and gas are not available past Big Pine, so plan ahead and come supplied. Take at least 3 liters of water per hiker for the summit push.

Drive slowly on White Mountain Road; carry a spare tire, and know how to use it. Marmots here have been known to chew through automobile wires and hoses, sometimes even disabling vehicles! Some motorists wrap their undercarriages with tarps to protect them.

This trailhead, hike, and summit are all high enough to give flatlanders splitting headaches if they have not acclimatized. Consider climbing this one after several days at elevation.

Climbers can acclimatize overnight at Grandview Campground, 5 miles north of the White Mountain Road turnoff and at 8,600 feet of elevation. The Barcroft Gate trailhead offers no facilities besides a toilet, but some climbers bivvy there prior to a summit hike. Either one offers campers a wondrous night of high-elevation stargazing.

CLIMBING THE MOUNTAIN

Hike north past the gate on the easily followed dirt road, passing White Mountain Research Center's Barcroft Station and Mount Barcroft to the west in about 2 miles. The names of both honor Sir Joseph Barcroft (1872–1947), a British physiologist who studied the effects of high altitude on the human body. An off-trail detour to the summit of Mount Barcroft (13,040 feet) adds only about 700 feet of climbing and 1 mile round-trip.

After Barcroft Station, our road climbs about 300 feet and passes a gate and Barcroft Observatory before stretching beside a long plateau. This alpine area supports 163 species of plants, including some found nowhere else in the world, though only a small number of them thrive above tree line where legions of marmots roam. You may also see herds of bighorn sheep; you will have to look carefully, as they blend into the rocks.

As you hike, marvel at the resourceful indigenous peoples who survived summers here by hunting and collecting plants. The Paiute consider the bighorn sheep sacred, called them *Nah Gah*, and hid while hunting them behind the stone stacks that are still visible.

White Mountain itself will occupy your view for the last several miles. Despite its name, the peak appears anything but white, except in winter. Rather, the volcanic rock projects a hue of brown, orange, and gray. Our final approach to the peak climbs switchbacks gaining about 1,000 feet in the last 2 miles. On the mountaintop stands a stone

Bristlecone pines can live for more than 4,000 years.

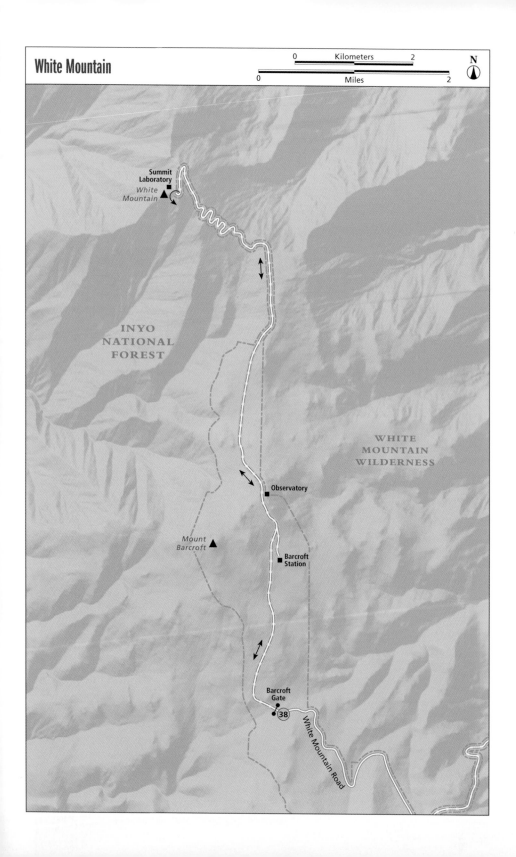

White Mountain

0 — Kilometers — 2

0 — Miles — 2

N

Summit
Laboratory
*White
Mountain*

INYO
NATIONAL
FOREST

WHITE
MOUNTAIN
WILDERNESS

Observatory

*Mount
Barcroft*

Barcroft
Station

Barcroft
Gate
38

White Mountain Road

research cabin where wind was once measured gusting at 162 miles per hour. Hang on to your hat as you enjoy the summit.

MILES AND DIRECTIONS

0.0 Hike north from Barcroft Gate (11,700 feet)

2.0 Reach Barcroft Station (12,450 feet) and continue north

7.5 Summit (14,252 feet)

15.0 Arrive back at the trailhead

HIGH HISTORY: ANCIENT TREES AND TRIBES

On this range stands Ancient Bristlecone Pine Forest, home to the world's oldest trees, some exceeding 4,000 years of age. Several Native American groups lived and walked along this range for many thousands of years. Archaeologists have discovered at least eleven villages above 10,000 feet of elevation. A cairn and oral history indicate that Paiutes summited White Mountain long before other groups arrived in California.

Construction on the first buildings and jeep road began in 1948. Since then, government scientists have studied physiology, physics, astronomy, and even missile technology here. The facilities also have hosted geology field camps and thousands of students since 1950.

Lone Pine Peak

39 **LONE PINE PEAK**

The mountain that looks so big and impressive from the town of Lone Pine is not Mount Whitney, as many wrongly assume, but Lone Pine Peak. Compared to its popular neighbor, this summit offers a shorter hike, fewer hikers, and no permit requirements for day use.

Distance: 10.4 miles (on trails and cross-country)
Time: 6 to 8 hours
Difficulty: Class 2; strenuous (for distance, elevation, and elevation gain)
Land agency: Inyo National Forest

Nearest facilities: Whitney Portal Store or Lone Pine
Trailhead elevation: 8,049 feet
Summit elevation: 12,949 feet
Elevation gain: 4,900 feet
Best season: June–Oct
Permits: None needed

FINDING THE TRAILHEAD

 From Lone Pine, drive toward Whitney Portal near the end of Whitney Portal Road. Look for a Meysan Lake trailhead parking sign just east of Whitney Portal Campground and park here.

CLIMBING THE MOUNTAIN

Be careful not to follow most hikers heading for Mount Whitney from its trailhead at the road's end. From the Meysan Lake trailhead parking area, walk south and east through the campground and follow the signs for about half a mile to Meysan Lake Trail; there will be a number of turns leading through the camp and past private cabins.

Our trail climbs steeply through the canyon above Meysan Creek, which will likely roar throughout your ascent. Enjoy the variety of trees as you gain elevation, passing Jeffrey pines, pinion pines, and finally, the rare and beautiful foxtail pines, which are native to the southeast Sierra and can live for more than 2,000 years. Admiring them provides a welcome diversion from the switchbacks.

After about 4 miles, our path levels off and we reach Grass Lake. The trail continues toward Meysan Lake, but our route leaves it here and continues cross-country. Hike south beside Grass Lake and turn to the southeast, aiming for a chute beneath the saddle between Lone Pine Peak and Peak 3985. Next comes the crux as we ascend the northwest-facing slope using that chute of talus and scree. This climb will test your strength but it also keeps the crowds away. Once you reach the saddle, the summit lies 0.6 mile to the northeast.

Looking over and far beyond John Muir Wilderness and Inyo National Forest, you will see one of the best views in the entire mountain range, including five of California's 14ers, including (from north to south) Mount Williamson, Mount Russell, Mount Whitney, Mount Muir, and Mount Langley.

MILES AND DIRECTIONS

0.0 Park beside Whitney Portal Road at the signed Meysan Lake trailhead lot and walk south and east through the campground, following signs for Meysan Lake Trail

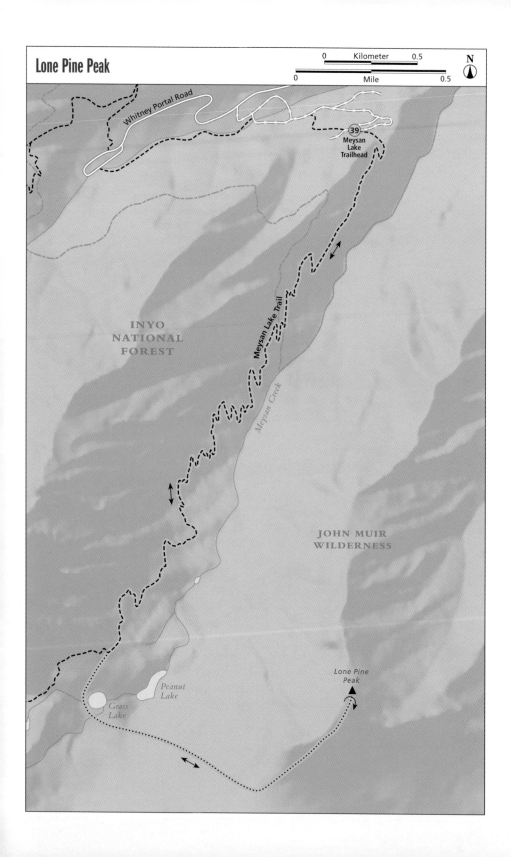

Lone Pine Peak

The recommended chute can be easy to miss on the descent; from the summit, it's the third one you will see to the southwest.

In late spring and early summer, use crampons to ascend snow on the northwest slope, which is much easier than scrambling up scree and talus later in the year.

If you decide to make an overnight trip, Grass Lake, Camp Lake, and Meysan Lake provide excellent camping sites (wilderness permit required).

0.5 At the Meysan Lake trailhead, hike south as the trail starts climbing

4.0 Leave the trail at Grass Lake, (10,876 feet) hiking cross-country or on a use trail to the southeast, then climb steeply to a saddle beside Lone Pine Peak

4.6 At the saddle (12,520 feet), hike northeast toward the summit

5.2 Summit (12,949 feet)

10.4 Arrive back at the trailhead

Mobius Arch frames Lone Pine Peak at dawn.

HIGH HISTORY: PAIUTE, A PINE, AND AN ALPINIST

The Paiute originally called the mountain *Opopago*. A pine tree growing near the Eastern Sierra community established in the 1860s inspired the name of the town, its nearby creek, and the mountain that towers above them both. A storm toppled the lone pine in 1876. Mountaineer Norman Clyde (1885–1972) made the first known ascent in 1925.

40 MATTERHORN PEAK

Matterhorn Peak, the highest peak in the northern Sierra, commands attention from miles around. Its north face, visible from Mono Village, appears steep and formidable, but its southeast flank features a nontechnical yet physically demanding summit route. If you're ready to gain more than 5,000 feet, here's a mountain that offers a high-elevation adventure.

Distance: 12 miles round-trip (on trails and cross-country)
Time: 8 to 10 hours
Difficulty: Class 3; strenuous (for distance, terrain, and elevation gain)
Land agency: Humboldt-Toiyabe National Forest

Nearest facilities: Mono Village
Trailhead elevation: 7,092 feet
Summit elevation: 12,279 feet
Elevation gain: 5,187 feet
Best season: June–Oct
Permits: None needed for day use

FINDING THE TRAILHEAD

Mono Village sits 15 miles southwest of Bridgeport at the end of Twin Lakes Road and at the edge of Humboldt-Toiyabe National Forest. The village sits on private property but allows hikers to use its parking lots. Find the lot beyond the bait shop and beside the marina. Our trail begins in its back right (southwest) corner.

CLIMBING THE MOUNTAIN

Pass the campground on your right and cross a wooden bridge, continuing south to the forest boundary and Horse Creek Trail bulletin board. Climb up switchbacks near the creek and through wooded terrain. After 2 miles, you will reach Horse Creek Meadow at 8,000 feet where you'll find a trail sign and junction. Instead of Cattle Creek Trail heading east, stay on Horse Creek Trail heading south.

Hike through pleasant woods beside the stream and enjoy early-season waterfalls. Eventually the trees give way to gravel and boulders. Stay on the left (east) side of Horse Creek as you negotiate several large talus fields. Refill water bottles before the route climbs above the stream; eventually the water runs only beneath the rocks. Beware, the first "pass" you see is false; the true top of this canyon lies beyond it. Several use trails may present themselves; it's best to stay close to the creek.

As you approach the true Horse Creek Pass, the use trail may be covered by snow. If not, you will have to ascend a long sandy slope. This is one of those two steps up, one step back kind of climbs that challenges the body and mind. Either way, you will have to navigate your own line to the summit. The regular route leads south past the mountain's steep eastern flank and ascends Class 2 and 3 terrain on the southeast slope. This is the crux of the climb, so it's a good thing you're tough!

Our summit view features Sawtooth Ridge to the northeast, Hoover Wilderness to the north, and Yosemite's high peaks to the south. Now you can tell your friends you climbed the Matterhorn! Whether you tell them it was the one in California rather than Europe is up to you.

Matterhorn Peak

Matterhorn Peak crowns Sawtooth Ridge.

MILES AND DIRECTIONS

0.0 From Mono Village, hike south on Horse Creek Trail

2.0 At Horse Creek Meadow, stay right (south)

6.0 Summit

12.0 Arrive back at the trailhead

HIGH HISTORY: "WILD EXULTATION," HERBERT HOOVER, AND JACK KEROUAC

Members of the Wheeler Survey named the mountain after the famous peak straddling Switzerland and Italy in 1878.

Lincoln Hutchinson, his brother James Hutchinson Jr., Charles Noble, and M. R. Dempster made the first known ascent on July 27, 1899. "The intense exhilaration of the climb, the noble grandeur of the scene, and the wild exultation of standing on a spot which, so far as we were aware, had never before felt the pressure of a human foot, combined to make up an experience never to be forgotten," Lincoln Hutchinson wrote.

MORE MOUNTAIN MATTERS

Some enjoy an outing this taxing more as an overnight trip. You can get a wilderness permit at the Forest Service office on Highway 395, 1 mile south of Bridgeport. Mono Village charges a fee for overnight parking.

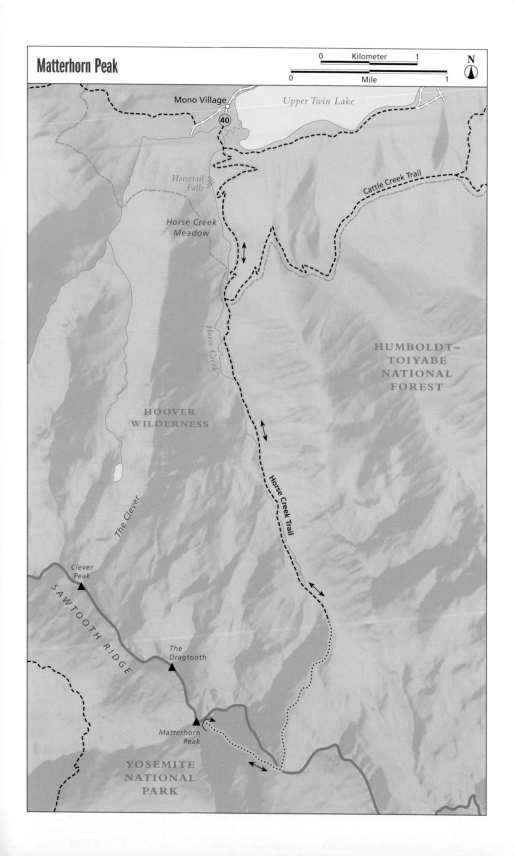

Matterhorn Peak

0 Kilometer 1

0 Mile 1

N

Mono Village

Upper Twin Lake

40

Horsetail Falls

Horse Creek Meadow

Cattle Creek Trail

Horse Creek

HUMBOLDT–
TOIYABE
NATIONAL
FOREST

HOOVER
WILDERNESS

Horse Creek Trail

The Clever

Clever Peak

SAWTOOTH RIDGE

The Dragtooth

Matterhorn Peak

YOSEMITE
NATIONAL
PARK

The Forest Service first protected this area in 1931, and it became official wilderness in 1964, named in honor of President Herbert Hoover.

Author Jack Kerouac wrote about climbing Matterhorn Peak in his 1958 novel *The Dharma Bums*, in which he (incorrectly) observed, "You can't fall off a mountain." Still, the book became popular among hippies in the 1960s and still inspires folks to climb the mountain today.

MORE MOUNTAINS IN THE EASTSIDE

J. DANTE PEAK

Distance: 0.8 mile round-trip (all on trails)
Time: 1 hour
Difficulty: Class 1; easy
Land agency: Death Valley National Park
Nearest facilities: Furnace Creek
Trailhead elevation: 5,454 feet
Summit elevation: 5,704 feet
Elevation gain: 250 feet
Best season: Year-round
Permits: None needed

Dante Peak

When a sheriff's deputy showed mine owners this vista in 1926, they named it for Italian poet Dante Alighieri, who described the nine circles of Hell in his *Divina Commedia*. Take Highway 190 through Death Valley between Furnace Creek and Death Valley Junction and then drive south on Dantes View Road to its end (this road occasionally closes in winter). The eastern landscape impresses, but for an even better view of Death Valley and the Panamint Range, hike north onto Dante Peak. The modest summit isn't marked on all maps, but the peak and its trail are clearly visible from the parking area.

K. TRAIL PEAK

Distance: 6.4 miles round-trip (on trails and cross-country)
Time: 3 to 4 hours
Difficulty: Class 2; moderate
Land agency: Inyo National Forest
Nearest facilities: Lone Pine
Trailhead elevation: 9,950 feet
Summit elevation: 11,617 feet
Elevation gain: 1,667 feet
Best season: June–Oct
Permits: None needed

Trail Peak

Members of the US Geological Survey in 1905 apparently named the mountain, which neighbors a historic trail that John Hockett pioneered in the 1860s. From Lone Pine, take Whitney Portal Road to Horseshoe Meadows Road and park at Horseshoe Meadow trailhead. Hike west to Trail Pass and turn right onto the Pacific Crest Trail. Then after half a mile, climb off-trail to your left (south) to the summit.

L. MOUNT GOULD

Distance: 10.2 miles (on trails and cross-country)
Time: 6 to 8 hours
Difficulty: Class 3; strenuous (for elevation, elevation gain, and terrain)
Land agency: Inyo National Forest
Nearest facilities: Independence
Trailhead elevation: 9,200 feet
Summit elevation: 13,005 feet
Elevation gain: 3,805 feet
Best season: June–Oct
Permits: None needed

Mount Gould

Joseph LeConte and others made the first recorded ascent in 1890. Four years later, LeConte climbed it again and named it after Wilson Gould who accompanied him. From Independence, drive west on Onion Valley Road for 13 miles to a large parking area. Hike west on Kearsarge Pass Trail for 4.6 miles, to Kearsarge Pass. Then take a use trail or scramble cross-country half a mile north to the blocky summit.

Burney Falls

Lassen Peak

NORTH STATE

For most people, climbing to the top of massive Mount Shasta delivers the thrill of a lifetime. Before Andrea Sansone and Andrew Hamilton even started, they had already climbed all fourteen of California's other 14ers, in just over seven days.

Smoky skies from a wildfire, deep sun cups in the snow, and enough fatigue to sideline almost anyone else all added to the difficulty. How did they manage 7,000 more feet of climbing?

"One step at a time," Sansone recalled.

High adventure beckons in the North State, as locals call it. The state's upper region includes seven northernmost counties, which contain about 400,000 people and some 28,000 square miles. Most of our outings fall within Shasta-Trinity National Forest and Lassen Volcanic National Park.

Volcanism defines the landscape, including Lassen Peak, which from 1914 to 1917 produced the most recent eruptions in California. More volcanoes abound, including Brokeoff Mountain, Cinder Cone, and Goosenest. These mountains form the southern end of the Cascade Range, which stretches as far north as Canada, as well as part of the volcanic Ring of Fire, which traces the west coast of North America and South America, and the east coast of Asia.

Perhaps the best known of California's volcanoes, Mount Shasta towers over Siskiyou County and attracts climbers from all over the world.

"I love Mount Shasta. It's such a unique mountain," Sansone said.

When Sansone and Hamilton summited on August 2, 2017, Sansone set a women's speed record by climbing all fifteen of California's 14ers in seven days, eleven hours, and twenty-two minutes, breaking the old mark by more than two days. She also topped her seventy-fourth and final 14er in the United States south of Canada, another rare feat.

"I have experienced more pain, suffering, and fear in these mountains than I ever had before, and yet at the same time, I feel a great sense of accomplishment," Sansone said. "These kinds of trips change you, teach you, and hopefully inspire others to get out and get into our mountains. I've learned more about myself in the mountains than anywhere else."

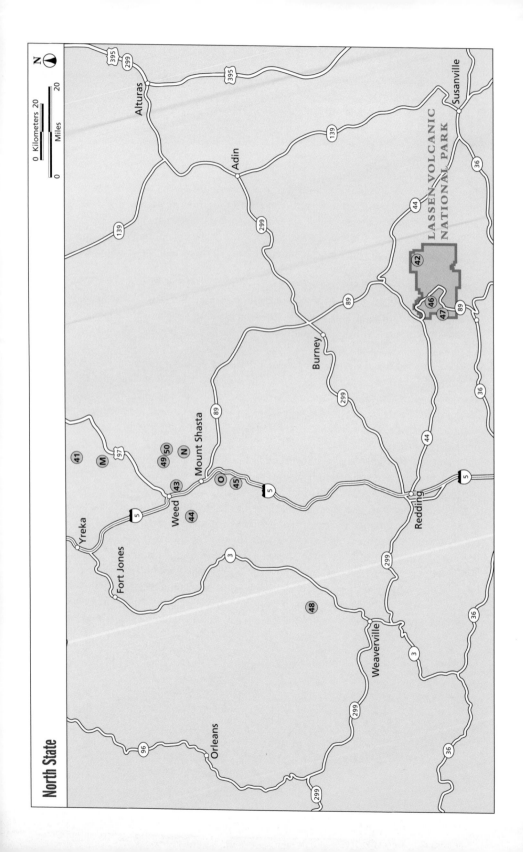

North State

North State Peaks at a Glance

SUMMIT	DISTANCE	DIFFICULTY	LAND AGENCY	SUMMIT ELEVATION	ELEVATION GAIN	BEST SEASON
41. Goosenest	2.8 miles	Class 1; easy to moderate	Klamath National Forest	8,280 feet	1,060 feet	May–Oct
42. Cinder Cone	4 miles	Class 2; moderate	Lassen Volcanic National Park	6,907 feet	846 feet	June–Oct
43. Black Butte	6.2 miles	Class 2; moderate	Shasta-Trinity National Forest	6,358 feet	1,858 feet	May–Oct
44. Mount Eddy	8 miles	Class 1; moderate	Shasta-Trinity National Forest	9,026 feet	2,576 feet	June–Oct
45. Castle Dome	5.2 miles	Class 1; moderate	Castle Crags State Park	4,906 feet	2,306 feet	March–Nov
46. Lassen Peak	5 miles	Class 2; moderate to strenuous	Lassen Volcanic National Park	10,457 feet	2,007 feet	July–Oct
47. Brokeoff Mountain	7 miles	Class 1; moderate to strenuous	Lassen Volcanic National Park	9,235 feet	2,600 feet	July–Oct
48. Granite Peak	11.6 miles	Class 1; strenuous	Shasta-Trinity National Forest	8,707 feet	4,084 feet	June–Oct
49. Shastina	10 miles	Class 3; strenuous	Shasta-Trinity National Forest	12,330	5,380	May–July
50. Mount Shasta	10 miles	Class 3; strenuous	Shasta-Trinity National Forest	14,179 feet	7,229 feet	May–July
M. Herd Peak	0.1 mile	Class 1; easy	Klamath National Forest	7,071 feet	21 feet	May–Nov
N. Gray Butte	3.3 miles	Class 1; easy	Shasta-Trinity National Forest	8,108 feet	665 feet	June–Oct
O. Mount Bradley	11 miles	Class 1; moderate	Shasta-Trinity National Forest	5,556 feet	1,224 feet	May–Oct

Goosenest

41 GOOSENEST

A seldom-visited but fascinating summit of the Cascades Range, Goosenest provides a look into the crater of a dormant volcano filled with trees, as well as a panoramic view of Klamath National Forest, Mount Shasta, and other Northern California peaks.

Distance: 2.8 miles round-trip (all on trails)
Time: 2 to 3 hours
Difficulty: Class 1; easy to moderate
Land agency: Klamath National Forest

Nearest facilities: Weed
Trailhead elevation: 7,220 feet
Summit elevation: 8,280 feet
Elevation gain: 1,060 feet
Best season: May–Oct
Permits: None needed

FINDING THE TRAILHEAD

 From the town of Weed, take Highway 97 northeast for 19.8 miles. Turn left (northwest) on Forest Road 45N22; this is a good place to reset your odometer. The dirt roads that lead to Goosenest are generally drivable for cars without high clearance.

At 2.9 miles from the highway turnoff, reach a Y and stay right. At 4.3 miles, reach a three-way junction and turn right. At 5.3 miles, reach a Y and stay right. At 6.5 miles, reach a Y and turn right. At 6.9 miles, reach a Y (where a hiking sign may be visible) and turn left, leaving 45N22 and turning onto 45N30. Stay on this road as it passes two gates until it reaches a quarry at 8.7 miles. Park beside the road here.

CLIMBING THE MOUNTAIN

Locate the trailhead north of the quarry and parking lot and hike north and then northeast through manzanita. Here the trail turns sharply to the west on a segment marked on some maps as Joe Rath Road, which steeply climbs the southern face and gains the crater rim. Red fir, white pine, and hemlock trees come into view.

When you gain the crater rim, the trail becomes fainter, but the route is simple enough. The shortest path to the summit follows the curve of the crater in a counterclockwise direction. The summit stands atop the eastern edge of the rim.

Our summit view includes Black Butte, Mount Eddy, Shasta Valley, Castle Crags, the Klamath Mountains, Mount McLoughlin, and, of course, Mount Shasta. Keep an eye out also for golden and bald eagles, which are present here year-round and especially abundant in winter.

> **MORE MOUNTAIN MATTERS**
> For an alternative route, use Forest Road 45N72 and park north of the mountain. A trail from here circles the mountain in a counterclockwise direction, climbs switchbacks on the western flank, and then joins the main route on the crater rim. This variation passes through the abundant trees on the northwest side of the volcano and adds about 1 mile.

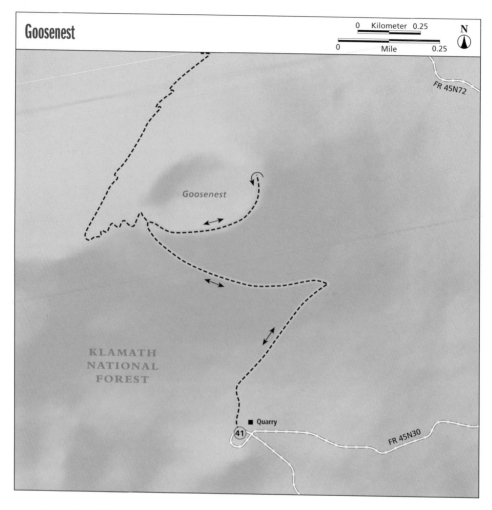

For variety, hikers can complete the loop around the crater or simply retrace their steps to descend.

MILES AND DIRECTIONS

0.0   From the quarry, hike north

0.5   Turn sharply left (west)

1.0   At crater rim trail junction, turn right (east)

1.3   Summit

2.6   Arrive back at the trailhead

Goosenest visitors can see much of the surrounding Klamath National Forest.

HIGH HISTORY: BIRDS' BREEDING BERTH

Goosenest is a dormant volcano that geologists believe is much younger than neighbors like Mount Shasta. Shasta and Modoc peoples (traditional enemies) occupied the area around it for millennia. The name dates back to 1874 and refers to both the abundant geese that migrate through this area (around 4 million per year) and the appearance of the crater, which resembles a giant nest. Klamath National Forest was established in 1905.

Cinder Cone

42 CINDER CONE

Explore the crater of a recently formed volcano on a short outing, with easy terrain leading to the cone and a strenuous climb to its rim. This unique adventure feels like visiting another world.

Distance: 4.0 miles round-trip (all on trails)	**Nearest facilities:** Old Station
	Trailhead elevation: 6,061 feet
Time: 2 to 3 hours	**Summit elevation:** 6,907 feet
Difficulty: Class 2; moderate	**Elevation gain:** 846 feet
Land agency: Lassen Volcanic National Park	**Best season:** June–Oct
	Permits: None needed

FINDING THE TRAILHEAD

From Highway 44 north of the park, take Butte Lake Road south for 6.5 miles to the day-use parking area beside Butte Lake. Look for a signed trailhead to the southwest.

CLIMBING THE MOUNTAIN

Hike southwest along a well-defined trail beside volcanic rock on our left. Our volcano's eruption produced these Fantastic Lava Beds, as well as the cinders covering our trail. Fire-scarred trees growing along the trail were not burned by Cinder Cone's eruption but by lightning-started fires that occurred more recently.

This path overlaps a portion of the Nobles Emigrant Trail, which William Nobles established in 1852 as a shorter alternative to Peter Lassen's route through these mountains.

As the Jeffrey pines thin, Cinder Cone comes into view. Our summit trail climbs visibly up its north slope. The route is steep and demanding as it climbs up loose scree, but it's not especially long, just about 0.3 mile from the base to the rim.

Our summit reveals a stunning panorama of the park's fascinating geology, including Lassen Peak, Prospect Peak, Snag Lake, and the Painted Dunes. But most unique is the look inside the crater itself, featuring giant rocky rings and even a few trees that amazingly grow in the hardened lava.

A walk around the crater's rim adds just a half-mile to the outing and shouldn't be missed. Those who want even more adventure can take a trail from the rim down into the crater itself.

MILES AND DIRECTIONS

- **0.0** Hike southwest from trailhead
- **0.5** Stay left (southwest) at Prospect Peak trail junction
- **1.5** Base of mountain
- **2.0** Summit
- **4.0** Arrive back at the trailhead

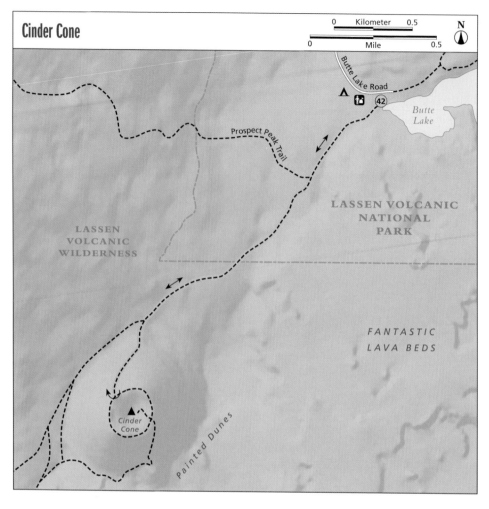

Cinder Cone

HIGH HISTORY: MOUNTAIN'S MYSTERIOUS MAKING

Gold Rush–era visitors estimated Cinder Cone's age to be just 25 years, but scientists debated and eventually increased that figure. By carbon-dating a tree engulfed and killed by the lava, a geologist estimated that the volcano formed in the 1650s. Although that

MORE MOUNTAIN MATTERS

A cinder cone is a kind of volcano formed by basaltic lava expelled from a single vent. Lava cools, solidifies, and breaks into cinders, which fall around the vent, creating a steep cone.

Butte Lake Road snows over and closes each winter and usually reopens by June.

While the author hesitates to describe this steep climb as "family-friendly," parents often take their kids on the hike up Cinder Cone.

A trail leads atop Cinder Cone and around its summit crater.

would make it more than twelve times older than earlier believed, Cinder Cone still qualifies as a baby by geologic standards.

President Teddy Roosevelt made this area Cinder Cone National Monument in 1907. After nearby Lassen Peak's multiple eruptions, starting in 1914, Congress created Lassen Volcanic National Park in 1916.

Black Butte

43 **BLACK BUTTE**

A path through a sea of dacite rock climbs to the summit of a volcanic plug dome. Though rough in places, the trail makes for a manageable ascent. This is a perfect warm-up for those adjusting to elevation and preparing for a Mount Shasta climb.

Distance: 6.2 miles round-trip (all on trails)
Time: 3 to 5 hours
Difficulty: Class 2; moderate
Land agency: Shasta-Trinity National Forest

Nearest facilities: Weed
Trailhead elevation: 4,500 feet
Summit elevation: 6,358 feet
Elevation gain: 1,858 feet
Best season: May–Oct
Permits: None needed

FINDING THE TRAILHEAD

From the town of Mount Shasta, drive northeast on Lake Street. The road merges briefly with northbound Washington Drive and then becomes Everitt Memorial Highway. Take this road north for 2.2 miles as it starts to climb and look for a Black Butte trailhead sign on your left. Turn left (west) onto Forest Road 41N18 but then turn quickly right (north) and drive for 1 mile. Turn left to drive straight toward the mountain. Then after 0.3 mile, turn right (north) again for about a mile. Turn left onto Forest Road 41N18A and drive another 0.6 mile to the trailhead.

CLIMBING THE MOUNTAIN

Hike west from the parking area through a forest of ponderosa pines, incense cedars, and firs. Then we reach the northern flank of the mountain, and our trail contours up large slopes of loose rock and scree. Our path curves and switches back a few times as it steadily climbs the north face. Soon you will clear tree line, and good views of the surrounding mountains become even better.

The final approach involves seven switchbacks leading to the summit area. There visitors will find the concrete foundation from the lookout station that stood until 1975. Surrounding views include Mount McLoughlin, Mount Eddy, and Castle Crags. Just 8 miles to the east, Mount Shasta looms large. If you weren't already inspired to climb Black Butte's parent peak, you could be now.

MILES AND DIRECTIONS

0.0 Hike west from the parking area toward the mountain's north face

1.8 Turn left (northeast) to stay on the trail at the first switchback

3.0 Climb the last seven switchbacks up the final slope

3.1 Summit

6.2 Arrive back at the trailhead

Black Butte

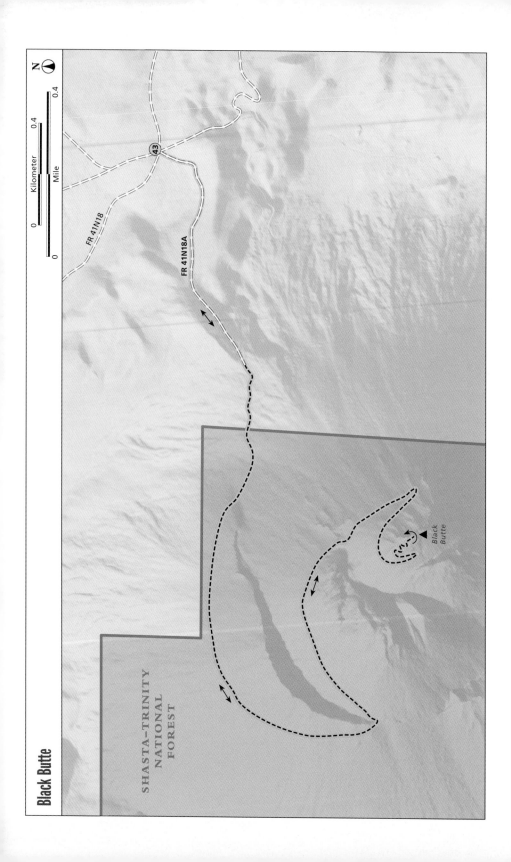

N

Kilometer
0   0.4

Mile
0   0.4

FR 41N18

FR 41N18A

43

SHASTA–TRINITY
NATIONAL
FOREST

Black
Butte

Trees thin out on the upper flanks of Black Butte.

HIGH HISTORY: "BLACK AS THE DARKEST IRON ORE"

This dome volcano formed at the base of Mount Shasta about 9,500 years ago. Batches of dacite lava welled up over hundreds of years, forming four domes, each larger than the one before. Today the volcano is extinct.

Miners called it Black Butte in the 1850s because it was "black as the darkest iron ore." Settlers later shifted its name to Wintoon Butte, then Cone Mountain, and then Black Butte once more, starting in 1934. The Forest Service built a fire lookout on the summit, the first in this region, in 1912. After a storm destroyed that structure in 1962, workers built a new one in 1963, which remained in use until 1973. A helicopter moved the building to a different location in 1975.

MORE MOUNTAIN MATTERS

Watch out for rattlesnakes, which are common here. To reduce the risk of a bite, it's a good idea to wear boots and long pants. For the same reason, you might want to leave your dog behind on this trip.

Black Butte's summit trail ascends the north face, which holds snow into mid-spring. Qualified climbers enjoy ascending in snowy conditions, which may require crampons and ice axes.

Mount Eddy

44 MOUNT EDDY

A moderate hike with a wide variety of scenery and terrain leads to the highest of the Klamath Mountains and perhaps the finest viewpoint in the North State. In terms of effort versus reward, this climb rates among California's best.

Distance: 8 miles round-trip (all on trails)	**Nearest facilities:** Mount Shasta
	Trailhead elevation: 6,450 feet
Time: 4 to 6 hours	**Summit elevation:** 9,026 feet
Difficulty: Class 1; moderate	**Elevation gain:** 2,576 feet
Land agency: Shasta-Trinity National Forest	**Best season:** June–Oct
	Permits: None needed

FINDING THE TRAILHEAD

From Interstate 5 about 3 miles north of Weed, exit at Edgewood/Gazelle. West of the freeway, turn right at the stop sign and drive northwest for 0.3 mile. Turn left on Stewart Springs Road and drive 4.7 miles. Then turn right onto Forest Route 42N17 / Parks Creek Road and drive about 11 miles, cresting Parks Creek Pass and parking at Deadfall Meadows Trailhead, where the road makes a hairpin turn.

CLIMBING THE MOUNTAIN

From Deadfall Meadows Trailhead, our path leads southeast through a grassy forest, crossing Deadfall Creek and other streams several times. Expect to get your feet wet, especially early in the season. Enjoy the colorful wildflowers that grow abundantly.

At 1.5 miles, Deadfall Lake Trail crosses Pacific Crest Trail at a saddle between the first two Deadfall Lakes. These are popular for fishing (brook, rainbow, and brown trout), swimming, and camping. Our route continues southeast.

Now we enter the glacially carved Deadfall Basin where more small but scenic lakes are found; our path traces the shores of two. Trees become scarcer, but look for rare foxtail pines, which grow here. The red face of Mount Eddy comes into full view to the east. Consider a break here before continuing toward our main attraction.

Hike briefly south and climb above tree line to gain the 8,000-foot Deadfall Summit atop a rocky ridge. Take a spur trail leading up switchbacks to the northeast. Our final approach gains about 1,000 feet as we climb through a sea of colorful rock.

From the highest point in Trinity County, you can see grand vistas of Trinity Alps, Castle Crags, Black Butte, Mount Shasta, and Deadfall Lakes.

> ### MORE MOUNTAIN MATTERS
> An alternate route starts at Parks Creek Trailhead, follows the PCT to the first of the Deadfall Lakes, and joins our featured trail from there. This adds a mile each way but avoids some 400 feet of climbing.

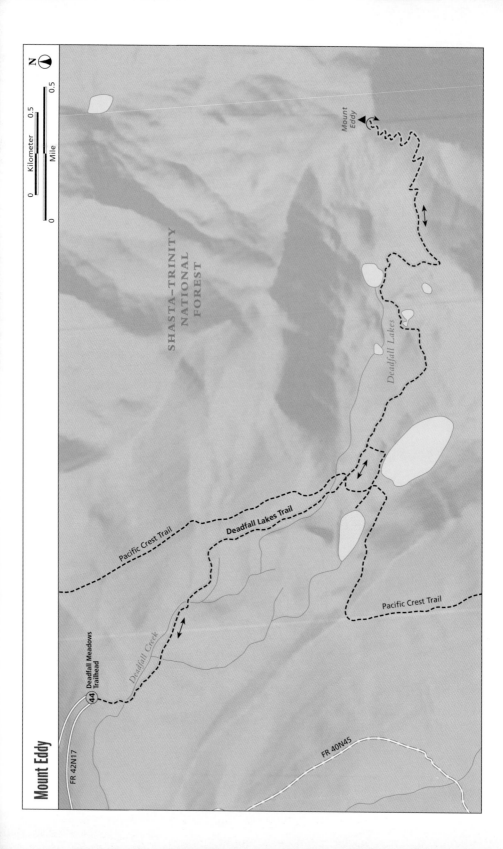

Mount Eddy

Deadfall Lakes and multiple North State summits highlight Mount Eddy's summit view.

MILES AND DIRECTIONS

0.0 From Deadfall Meadows Trailhead, hike southeast on Deadfall Lakes Trail

1.5 At PCT junction, continue southeast

3.0 At Deadfall Summit (8,000 feet), turn left (north) to ascend summit spur trail

4.0 Summit (9,026 feet)

8.0 Arrive back at the trailhead

HIGH HISTORY: SIGNIFYING SHASTA'S WONDER WOMAN

The Wintu called this peak *Num-mel-be-le-sas-pam*, or "west blaze mountain." The mountain's current name apparently honors Olive Eddy (1834–1909). Some sources say she was the first woman to climb Mount Shasta in 1856, though others say she was the first woman to climb her namesake mountain in the 1880s. Still others say her husband Nelson Eddy (1830–1921) inspired the mountain's name. A fire lookout operated here from 1912 to 1931; Hallie Daggett, the first woman to staff a Forest Service lookout, kept a stoic watch there for fourteen years. A donation helped the Forest Service purchase 3,000 acres on its northern face in 2014, ensuring continued public access.

Castle Dome

45 CASTLE DOME

A striking land of jagged granite peaks commands attention from those traveling through the North State on Interstate 5. A steep but well-traveled trail takes hikers into the heart of the stone towers and to the shoulder of Castle Dome. Reaching the dome's summit requires about 250 feet of Class 4 and 5 climbing.

Distance: 5.2 miles round-trip (all on trails)
Time: 3 to 4 hours
Difficulty: Class 1 (to the dome's base); moderate
Land Agencies: Castle Crags State Park

Trailhead elevation: 2,600 feet
Summit elevation: 4,906 feet
Elevation gain: 2,306 feet
Best season: March–Nov
Permits: None needed

FINDING THE TRAILHEAD

Castle Crags State Park lies beside Interstate 5, 6 miles south of Dunsmuir or 48 miles north of Redding. Take exit 724 and drive west on Castle Creek Road for a quarter-mile. Turn right to enter the park and you will quickly see a visitor center on the right; you can self-register and pay your entrance fee here. Then turn right onto Vista Point Road and drive about 2 miles to the parking lot at the road's end.

CLIMBING THE MOUNTAIN

From the parking lot, take Castle Dome Trail (which initially overlaps Root Creek Trail) leading west for about 0.3 mile. Then turn left to stay on Castle Dome Trail. Soon you will cross the Pacific Crest Trail. At a junction with Bob's Hat Trail, turn right. All the while you will gain elevation as you climb steeply up switchbacks through a lush pine forest.

Climbing eases near the turnoff for Indian Springs. The only source of water on the trail, the springs lie a quarter-mile to the west and provide a welcome break on hot days. Refill bottles if needed; there's little shade from here on.

Now our trail climbs above the thick forest, and vistas improve as Mount Shasta and Castle Dome come into view. The trail leaves the state park and enters Castle Crags Wilderness within Shasta-Trinity National Forest. Jagged granite pinnacles beside the trail hint at the scenery to come. The final stretch of the trail curves through manzanita before ending atop a saddle.

> ### MORE MOUNTAIN MATTERS
> Consider a winter visit. These granite formations are even more spectacular when snow covers their peaks.
> The vista point east of the parking lot makes a short and worthy detour.
> Rock climbers should take a look at Mount Hubris, just west of Castle Dome, which features Cosmic Wall, a fabulous 5.6 route that's among the best in the North State.

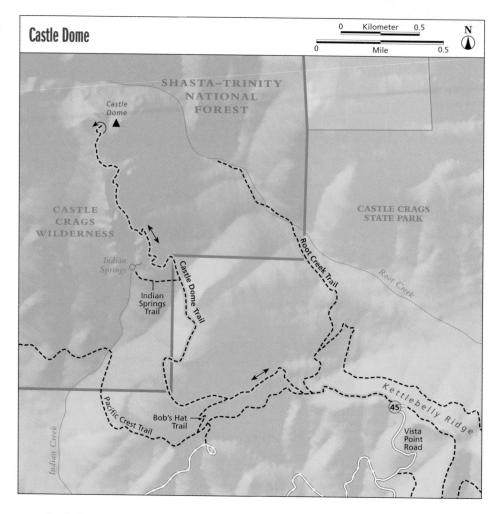

Castle Dome

Castle Dome stands due east, though ascending the last few hundred feet to its summit requires Class 5 rock-climbing technique. However, that's not necessary to enjoy the grand perspective of Castle Crags, which you have earned.

MILES AND DIRECTIONS

0.0 From the parking lot, hike west on Castle Dome Trail

0.3 Turn left (west) to stay on Castle Dome Trail

0.4 At Pacific Crest Trail junction, go straight (west)

0.8 At Bob's Hat Trail junction, go right (west)

1.5 At Indian Springs Trail junction, stay right (north)

2.6 Trail ends beside Castle Dome

5.2 Return to start

A Castle Dome hike features the striking scenery of Castle Crags State Park.

HIGH HISTORY: MALARIA, MINERS, AND MODOCS

Castle Crags' granite peaks formed 170 million years ago as a result of tectonic plate movement followed by glacier carving and erosion. Okwanuchu Shasta made their home here and believed that spirits lived in the rocky spires. Neighboring Wintu, Achumawi, and Modoc considered the peaks sacred as well.

European American explorers and trappers arrived in the 1820s, bringing with them a malaria epidemic that wiped out most of the Okwanuchu Shasta by 1833. The Gold Rush brought thousands of miners to the North State, and a false rumor of gold drew them to Castle Crags specifically in 1853. The miners' pursuit of gold muddied rivers and streams to the point that the salmon run failed, leaving indigenous people without food. When miners attacked Modocs for stealing flour, the Battle of Castle Crags erupted in 1855.

California purchased 925 acres to make a state park in 1933. Some 220 men from the Civilian Conservation Corps arrived that same year to build the park's roads, trails, and buildings. Construction of Interstate 5 in 1959 led to the demolition of most CCC-era structures. Congress passed the California Wilderness Act in 1984, which established the 12,232-acre Castle Crags Wilderness within Shasta-Trinity National Forest.

Lassen Peak

46 **LASSEN PEAK**

A steep, switchbacked trail leads to the summit of a historic volcano. Climbing quickly over tree line, the well-traveled path leads up the mountain's southeastern ridge to an awesome overview of a lava-formed land. This might be the North State's best payoff for a half-day climb.

Distance: 5 miles round-trip (all on trails)
Time: 3 to 5 hours
Difficulty: Class 2; moderate to strenuous (for elevation gain)
Land agency: Lassen Volcanic National Park

Nearest facilities: Kohm Yah-mah-nee Visitor Center
Trailhead elevation: 8,450 feet
Summit elevation: 10,457 feet
Elevation gain: 2,007 feet
Best season: July–Oct
Permits: None needed

FINDING THE TRAILHEAD

From the southern entrance to the park, drive about 7 miles north on Highway 89. From the western entrance station, drive about 23 miles southeast on Highway 89. The trailhead parking area is about a mile northeast of Lake Helen on the north side of the road.

CLIMBING THE MOUNTAIN

Our trail leads north from the parking area, climbing up a ridge, making a few sharp turns, and then leading northeast. After about a half-mile, the path clears tree line and arrives at the base of the mountain's southeast flank. Now we ascend switchbacks up slopes that often appear barren, although sharp-eyed hikers may spot rare wildflowers in season. For instance, the Lassen smelowskia grows in this area and nowhere else on Earth. Spare a moment to appreciate the beautiful and impressively tough alpine plants that survive here.

After about 2 miles, we reach the summit crater. Steam eruptions began hurling rocks from here in 1914. Then lava filled the crater in 1915 before another steam blast showered dacite rock around the mountain. From here, our trail continues northeast along a ridge toward the summit block. A short scramble will take you to its highest point.

Brokeoff Mountain to the southwest, Reading Peak to the east, and Loomis Peak to the west highlight our view. You might also see massive Mount Shasta about 75 miles to the northwest.

MILES AND DIRECTIONS

0.0   Hike north from the trailhead on Lassen Peak Trail

2.0   From the southern edge of the crater, hike northeast along the ridge

2.5   Summit

5.0   Arrive back at the trailhead

Lassen Peak marks the highest point of Shasta County.

This mountain is the southernmost active volcano in the Cascade Range and the largest lava dome on Earth. A lava dome is formed by masses of thick lava that pile over and around a volcanic vent.

Skiers willing to earn their turns enjoy descending Lassen Peak. As the upper portions of Highway 89 close with the first heavy snowfall, this requires a long approach in winter and early spring, but some find good snow for a short period after the road reopens in late spring or early summer.

HIGH HISTORY: "FULL OF FIRE"

Lassen Peak arose from the now-collapsed Brokeoff Volcano 27,000 years ago. Indigenous peoples including the Atsugewi, Maidu, Yahi, and Yana used the area as a meeting point during summer months for millennia, calling the mountain *Waganupa*.

California's Gold Rush brought the first large numbers of European Americans, including immigrant and future namesake Peter Lassen (1800–1859), who pioneered a trail and guided settlers here. Grover Godfrey led the first known ascent in 1851, writing, "The sight is unrivaled in beauty and magnificence. It's like the vision of some dream land." Helen Tanner Brodt made the first known female ascent in 1864.

Climbers celebrate reaching the summit of Lassen Peak.

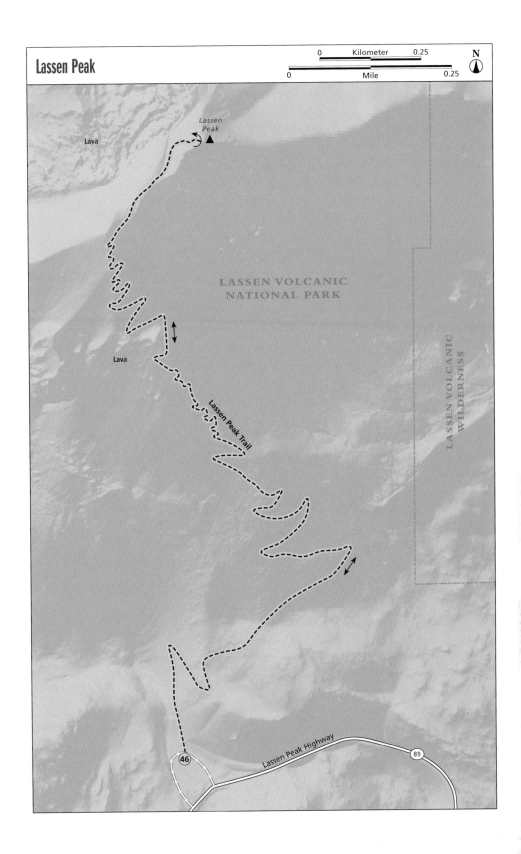

Lassen Peak

Lava

Lassen Peak

LASSEN VOLCANIC
NATIONAL PARK

Lava

Lassen Peak Trail

LASSEN VOLCANIC
WILDERNESS

Lassen Peak Highway

46

89

0   Kilometer   0.25

0   Mile   0.25

N

President Theodore Roosevelt protected the area as a national monument in 1907. Native Americans had warned that Lassen "was full of fire and water, and that one day the mountain would blow itself to pieces." The volcano proved them right with a series of discharges between 1914 and 1916, especially on May 22, 1915, when an explosion hurled rock high into the air, devastating nearby areas and raining ash up to 280 miles away. The eruptions attracted national interest and led Congress to create Lassen Volcanic National Park in 1916.

47 BROKEOFF MOUNTAIN

Hike through a vibrant forest on your way to the alpine summit of an ancient volcano. Less popular than Lassen Peak, this hike boasts more trees, wildflowers, and wildlife than the park's namesake mountain.

Distance: 7 miles round-trip (all on trails)
Time: 4 to 6 hours
Difficulty: Class 1; moderate to strenuous
Land agency: Lassen Volcanic National Park

Nearest facilities: Kohm Yah-mah-nee Visitor Center
Trailhead elevation: 6,635 feet
Summit elevation: 9,235 feet
Elevation gain: 2,600 feet
Best season: July–Oct
Permits: None needed

FINDING THE TRAILHEAD

From the park's southern border, drive north on Highway 89 for 0.5 mile. From Kohm Yah-mah-nee Visitor Center, drive south on Highway 89 for 0.5 mile. Park just south of the entrance station on the east side of the road.

Brokeoff Mountain rises above multiple other peaks that were once part of the massive Brokeoff Volcano.

Brokeoff Mountain

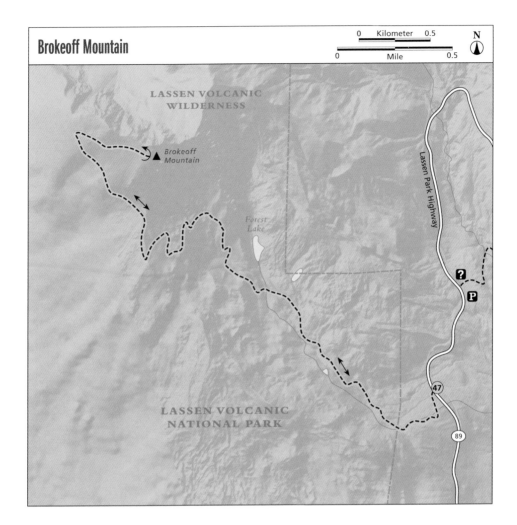

Brokeoff Mountain

CLIMBING THE MOUNTAIN

Our adventure begins at a signed trailhead on the west side of Highway 89. The trail leads briefly south and then curves to the northwest through a forest of pines, firs, and hemlocks. The trail crosses several streams and marshes in the first 2 miles. Bird-watchers may spot juncos, chickadees, and flycatchers. Abundant wildflowers on the trail peak in July and August.

After the trail passes south of Forest Lake, we climb above tree line and into a world of volcanic rock and sky, and the trail becomes steeper in places.

MORE MOUNTAIN MATTERS

With a generally accessible trailhead, Brokeoff Mountain attracts skiers and snowshoers in spring.

Brokeoff Mountain is the second-highest summit in the park and the highest summit in Tehama County.

Traverse westward beneath the southeast face of the mountain, northwest to the summit ridge, and finally east to the summit area.

As you catch your breath, take a look around and consider the natural history that surrounds you. Lassen Peak to the northeast formed 27,000 years ago. In contrast, much of what you see to the east was part of the same massive Brokeoff Volcano half a million years ago. May the aged wonders around you make you feel young in comparison as you bid them farewell and descend.

MILES AND DIRECTIONS

0.0   From the signed trailhead, hike south and then northwest

1.2   Cross a marshy stream south of Forest Lake

3.5   Summit

7.0   Arrive back at the trailhead

HIGH HISTORY: COLLAPSED CALDERA MAKES MODERN MOUNTAIN

This peak is the highest remaining point of the enormous Brokeoff Volcano, which is also called Mount Tehama. The volcano erupted numerous times between 400,000 and 600,000 years ago and once stood some 11 miles wide and 11,500 feet tall before its caldera collapsed. Nearby Mount Conard, Pilot Pinnacle, Mount Diller, and Diamond Peak are also remnants of Brokeoff Volcano.

48 GRANITE PEAK

A challenging, physical climb pays off with a spectacular view of the Trinity Alps Wilderness, Trinity Lake, and the Cascades. This guide recommends the Stoney Ridge route, which is a few miles longer but less steep than Granite Peak Trail.

Distance: 11.6 miles round-trip (all on trails)
Time: 6 to 8 hours
Difficulty: Class 1; strenuous (for distance and elevation gain)
Land agency: Shasta-Trinity National Forest

Nearest facilities: Trinity Center
Trailhead elevation: 4,623 feet
Summit elevation: 8,707 feet
Elevation gain: 4,084 feet
Best season: June–Oct
Permits: None needed

FINDING THE TRAILHEAD

Take Highway 3 north of Weaverville. A half-mile east of Trinity Alps Road, or 3 miles west of Granite Peak Road, turn northwest onto Forest Road 35N73Y, marked by a Stoney Ridge trailhead sign. This dirt road is generally drivable for low-clearance vehicles. Drive about 6 miles to a parking area. The signed trail begins to the north.

CLIMBING THE MOUNTAIN

Stoney Ridge Trail leads north through a conifer forest. Douglas firs, incense cedars, and sugar pines line our path for most of our journey. Admiring them might take your mind off the abundant climbing on our agenda.

As we climb Stoney Ridge, the trail crests a clearing and our destination comes into view to the north. From this elevation, Granite Peak appears to be a large, tree-covered hill. But the higher one climbs, the more visible its rocky summit becomes.

By the wilderness boundary, the path delves into thicker trees once more and the switchbacks begin in earnest. The trail crosses streams a few times and parallels Stoney Creek.

Keep an eye out for a use trail splitting off to the right (northeast) around the forty-third switchback. If you reach Stonewall Pass, you've overshot it and should turn around to find it. This less-traveled path crosses Stoney Creek and climbs steeply once more while traversing the mountain's southern ridge. The use trail isn't always obvious, so

---

MORE MOUNTAIN MATTERS

Though this guide recommends Stoney Ridge Trail, Granite Peak Trail provides a shorter but steeper option. Granite Peak Road accesses this 7.4-mile outing that climbs some 4,500 feet.

Red Mountain Meadow provides another attractive camping spot and a base for ascending nearby Red Mountain and Middle Peak.

Granite Peak

navigate carefully. We climb above tree line and into a world of rock and sky as the route joins the main Granite Peak Trail. The developing views merely hint at what's to come. From the trail junction, just a half-mile separates you from the summit to the northwest.

When you make the final turn, you will understand why hikers rave about this peak and work so hard to reach it. Jaw-dropping vistas stand out in every direction. Trinity Lake sprawls to the east. Red Mountain, Little Granite Peak, and Sawtooth Mountain appear to the west. Dozens of features from the Trinity Alps surround you, and both Mount Shasta and Lassen Peak loom in the distance. One can see why some hikers enjoy spending a night atop this mountain. At the least, stay a while to enjoy the views you have earned.

MILES AND DIRECTIONS

- 0.0 Hike north on Stoney Ridge Trail
- 1.3 Trinity Alps Wilderness boundary
- 3.9 Turn right (northeast) onto use trail
- 5.3 Turn left (northwest)
- 5.8 Summit
- 11.6 Arrive back at the trailhead

Granite Peak climbers earn a rewarding view of Trinity Alps.

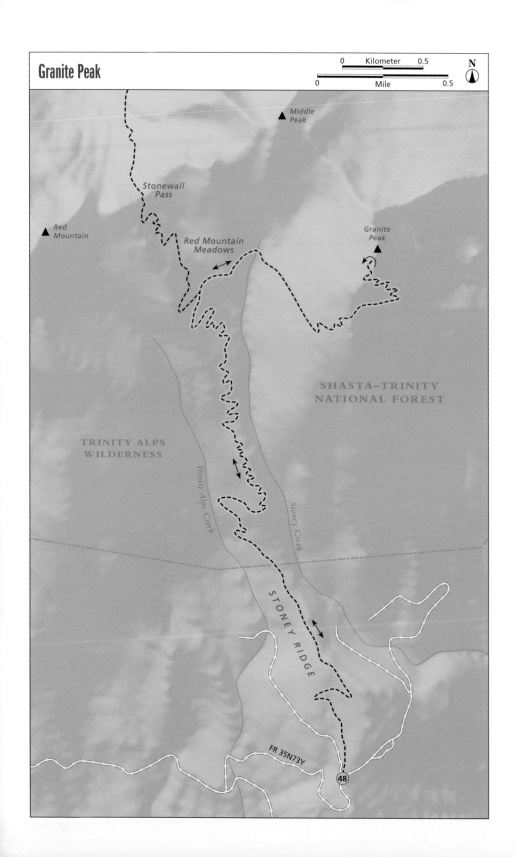

Granite Peak

0   Kilometer   0.5
0   Mile   0.5

N

Middle
Peak

Stonewall
Pass

Red
Mountain

Red Mountain
Meadows

Granite
Peak

SHASTA–TRINITY
NATIONAL FOREST

TRINITY ALPS
WILDERNESS

Trinity Alps Creek

Stoney Creek

STONEY RIDGE

FR 35N73Y

48

HIGH HISTORY: GEOGRAPHIC GAFFE MAKES MOUNTAINS' MONIKER

Wintu Indians occupied this area prior to the arrival of European Americans and the Gold Rush. A pioneer named Pierson Reading named Trinity River in 1845 because he thought it flowed into Trinidad Bay. Though he was mistaken, the name stuck, and others later extended it to Trinity County and its mountains. Anna and Anton Webber opened Trinity Alps Resort in 1922, applying the name of the Austrian Alps, which they admired, to these peaks.

Salmon-Trinity Alps Primitive Area was created in the 1930s, later to become Trinity Alps Wilderness. The California Wilderness Act of 1984 nearly doubled its size, now 517,000 acres.

Shastina

49 SHASTINA

Though it stands as the third tallest of all the Cascades volcanoes, Shastina sees fewer than 1 percent as many visitors as neighboring Mount Shasta. Those who overlook the little sister miss out because it provides a first-rate adventure, a manageable day trip, and a good trial run before tackling the taller mountain.

Distance: 10 miles round-trip (on trails and cross-country)
Time: 8 to 10 hours
Difficulty: Class 3; strenuous (for distance and elevation gain)
Land agency: Shasta-Trinity National Forest

Nearest facilities: Mount Shasta (city)
Trailhead elevation: 6,950 feet
Summit elevation: 12,330 feet
Elevation gain: 5,380 feet
Best season: May–July
Permits: Required

FINDING THE TRAILHEAD

From the town of Mount Shasta, drive northeast on Lake Street. The road merges briefly with northbound Washington Drive and then becomes Everitt Memorial Highway. Drive about 12 miles to Bunny Flat Trailhead and park beside the road.

PLANNING AND PREPARATION

All climbers should carry human waste bags, summit passes, and wilderness permits. These are available at trailheads and at Mount Shasta Ranger Station (in the city of Mount Shasta).

You will find the best conditions here in the early season; ascending snow above Hidden Valley easily beats climbing loose rock and scree. You will need an ice ax and crampons.

CLIMBING THE MOUNTAIN

Locate the trail to Horse Camp north of the road beside the outhouses. A well-traveled path leads to Horse Camp, though snow may cover it as low as Bunny Flat; be prepared to navigate with map and compass.

At Horse Camp stands rustic Shasta Alpine Lodge, a Sierra Club shelter built in 1923, which deserves a visit. You will find campsites, outhouses, and water here.

Most traffic from the lodge heads northeast up Avalanche Gulch, but the path to Shastina leads north toward Hidden Valley. Snowfields may obscure the trail in places early in the season. Climb gradually as the route clears tree line.

Hidden Valley occupies a large plateau, attracting campers bound for both Shastina and Mount Shasta. Beyond it, climbing resumes and becomes steeper, so put on your crampons if needed. Ascend Cascade Gulch to the north between Shastina and Mount Shasta, climbing to the saddle between the two mountains. This segment gains elevation rapidly, so take it slowly. From the saddle, climb west to the summit block, which features a small amount of Class 3 climbing.

Shastina summit visitors can see inside its crater and view frozen Clarence King Lake.

Not only does the peak afford views of Castle Crags, Mount Eddy, and Mount Shasta, but it also overlooks Shastina's fascinating summit crater, containing Clarence King Lake and other small bodies of bright blue water.

Exercise caution on the descent, especially late in the season when rockfall is a greater hazard. If glissading (simply put, this means sliding down the snow on your butt), be sure to remove your crampons, avoid ice, and steer clear of exposed rock. Only attempt this if you have an ice axe and the ability to use it to arrest your descent.

MILES AND DIRECTIONS

0.0 From Bunny Flat Trailhead, hike north on the trail toward Horse Camp

0.2 At trail junction, turn left (west)

0.5 At trail junction, turn right (north)

1.7 Reach Horse Camp (7,884 feet) and hike north toward Hidden Valley

2.9 Reach Hidden Valley (9,200 feet) and climb north up Cascade Gulch

4.7 At the saddle (11,900 feet) between Mount Shasta and Shastina, climb left (west) toward Shastina's summit

5.0 Summit (12,330 feet)

10.0 Arrive back at the trailhead

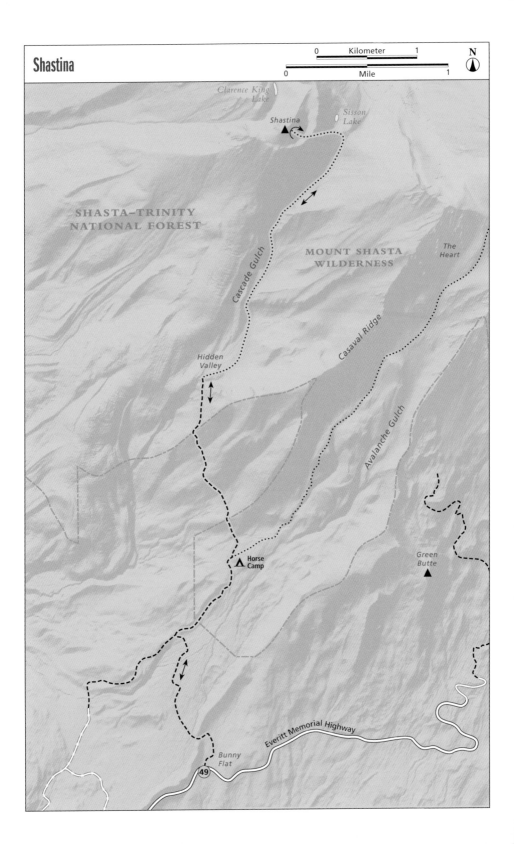

Shastina

Clarence King Lake

Sisson Lake

Shastina

SHASTA-TRINITY
NATIONAL FOREST

Cascade Gulch

MOUNT SHASTA
WILDERNESS

The Heart

Hidden Valley

Casaval Ridge

Avalanche Gulch

Horse Camp

Green Butte

Everitt Memorial Highway

Bunny Flat

49

N

0   Kilometer   1

0   Mile   1

HIGH HISTORY: SHASTA SPAWNS A SISTER

An eruption of Mount Shasta around 9,500 years ago formed the Shastina satellite cone west of the higher and older mountain.

Clarence King Lake in the summit crater is named for a nineteenth-century government geologist who surveyed Yosemite and explored the Sierra Nevada Range. King (1842–1901) climbed Shastina in 1870 and documented Mount Shasta's glaciers. He also has mountains named after him in California, Utah, and Antarctica.

50 **MOUNT SHASTA**

The North State's highest summit provides a world-class climbing experience. The most commonly ascended John Muir Route up Avalanche Gulch requires mountaineering skills, altitude acclimatization, and a high level of fitness, but rewards successful climbers in proportion to the mountain's challenge. Summiting Mount Shasta marks a lifetime achievement for many climbers.

Distance: 10 miles round-trip (on trails and cross-country)
Time: 1 to 2 days
Difficulty: Class 3; strenuous (for distance and elevation gain)
Land agency: Shasta-Trinity National Forest

Nearest facilities: Mount Shasta (city)
Trailhead elevation: 6,950 feet
Summit elevation: 14,179 feet
Elevation gain: 7,229 feet
Best season: May–July
Permits: Required for day use and overnight travel

FINDING THE TRAILHEAD

From the town of Mount Shasta, drive northeast on Lake Street. The road merges briefly with northbound Washington Drive and then becomes Everitt Memorial Highway. Drive about 12 miles to Bunny Flat Trailhead and park beside the road.

PLANNING AND PREPARATION

Mount Shasta requires more preparation than other summits described in this book. For starters, all climbers should bring and know how to use both ice axes and crampons. Helmets are strongly encouraged. If needed, The Fifth Season mountain shop in the city of Mount Shasta offers sales, rentals, and good advice.

When to go? Most climbers want to go from April through June, and possibly July after a big winter. Some ambitious skiers make winter and early-spring ascents and enjoy glorious turns down the mountain, but they face short days and avalanche hazards; this is an experts-only proposition. Late-summer and fall climbers must ascend more loose rock and scree and face greater rockfall hazards. This guide suggests staying within the late-spring window; climbing Mount Shasta in peak season with optimum conditions still provides plenty of challenge for almost everyone.

One day or two? A single-day ascent allows climbers to carry less gear. Those choosing this option must arrive with an extra-high level of fitness, ready to gain 7,230 feet in one push and climb for 12 straight hours or more. In contrast, a two-day ascent requires heavier packs and overnight gear but allows for a slower pace. This better suits those with less high-and-fast climbing prowess. Be advised: Those spending a night on the mountain should bring sturdy tents (at least three-season shelters) that can withstand major storms and fierce winds, which can occur here even in summer.

Either way, all climbers should carry human waste bags, and those exceeding 10,000 feet will need summit passes. Overnight and one-day climbers are required to obtain free wilderness permits. These are available at trailheads and Mount Shasta Ranger Station (in the city of Mount Shasta).

Words of caution: Ascending Mount Shasta poses a greater challenge and involves more risk than other climbs in this book. Prepare and plan adequately; this should not be your first big mountain. Also, be advised that multiple accidents and rescues occur on Mount Shasta every year. When facing bad weather, turning back is a better choice than continuing.

CLIMBING THE MOUNTAIN

One-day climbers commonly start from Bunny Flat around midnight. Two-day parties could reasonably start their first day in mid-morning. Locate the trail to Horse Camp north of the road beside the outhouses. A well-traveled path leads to Horse Camp and beyond, though snow may cover it as low as Bunny Flat. Early-season climbers especially should be prepared to navigate with map and compass.

At Horse Camp stands rustic Shasta Alpine Lodge, a Sierra Club shelter built in 1923, which deserves a visit on your way up the mountain. Campsites, outhouses, and water are available, and knowledgeable caretakers staff the lodge in summer.

Then our path leads northeast up Avalanche Gulch as the climbing begins in earnest. As its name suggests, this is the site of frequent snowslides; winter and early-spring visitors should avoid it after heavy storms and exercise caution at other times. Spring and summer climbers may need crampons here. This segment, called Olberman's Causeway, features a stone-lined path that's visible in late season. Continue up switchbacks as the route climbs above tree line.

Helen Lake marks roughly the halfway point of elevation between Bunny Flat and the summit. The only flat space for miles, this is where overnight climbers pitch their tents. Snow often covers the small lake, so be prepared to melt snow for water. Most parties start from here well before dawn on the second day, leaving their overnight gear to retrieve on the descent.

Crampons and ice axes are essential for the next segment, which leads up and right of The Heart (an aptly named rock formation). At up to 35 degrees, this marks the steepest part of the climb, so take your time. Early-season climbers typically aim northeast for the notch between Red Banks (a horizontal strip of volcanic stone) and Thumb Rock. However, a crevasse forms here later in the season, leading climbers to instead ascend through a gap in Red Banks. At around 12,800 feet is a good place to take a break, because another challenge follows.

That would be Misery Hill, which deserves its name—and not just because it climbs about 1,000 feet in thin air. The slope also presents a false summit, so don't be discouraged to discover more climbing beyond it. Instead, take heart from its top, because the true summit has finally come into sight, less than a half-mile and just 330 vertical feet away.

From the top, enjoy your hard-earned view of Lassen Peak, Mount Eddy, Mount McLoughlin, and many more summits in the North State and Southern Oregon.

Exercise caution on the descent, especially late in the season when rockfall is a greater hazard. If glissading, be sure to remove your crampons, avoid ice, and steer clear of exposed rock.

Mount Shasta

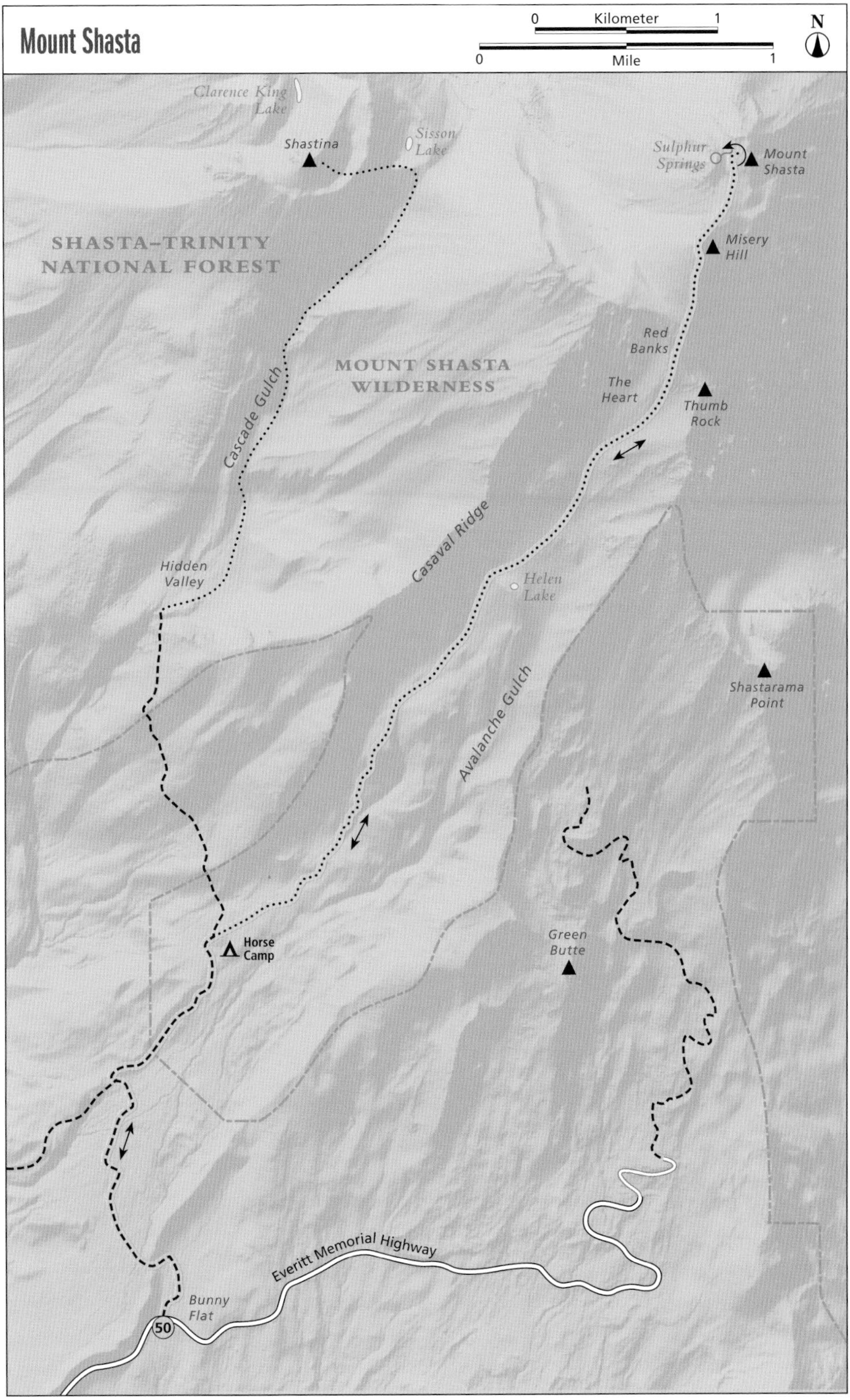
0 Kilometer 1
0 Mile 1
N
Clarence King Lake
Sisson Lake
Shastina
Sulphur Springs
Mount Shasta
SHASTA–TRINITY NATIONAL FOREST
Misery Hill
Red Banks
MOUNT SHASTA WILDERNESS
The Heart
Thumb Rock
Cascade Gulch
Casaval Ridge
Hidden Valley
Helen Lake
Avalanche Gulch
Shastarama Point
Horse Camp
Green Butte
Everitt Memorial Highway
Bunny Flat
50

MILES AND DIRECTIONS

0.0 From Bunny Flat Trailhead, hike north on the trail toward Horse Camp

0.2 At trail junction, turn left (west)

0.5 At trail junction, turn right (north)

1.7 Reach Horse Camp (7,884 feet) and continue northeast toward Avalanche Gulch

3.2 Reach Helen Lake (10,443 feet), the most commonly used overnight spot; continue northeast toward Thumb Rock

4.2 Climb left (west) of Thumb Rock, past Red Banks (12,800 feet), and start Misery Hill

4.7 Reach the top of Misery Hill (13,850 feet) and continue northeast to summit

5.0 Summit (14,180 feet)

10.0 Return to start

HIGH HISTORY: "COMELY AND PERFECT"

Great Spirit made a hole in the sky and piled snow and ice high enough to make a mountain so tall that it pierced the clouds, according to Native American beliefs. "It was made before any other mountain in the world," they say. Great Spirit added rivers, creeks, trees, birds, fish, bears, and other animals. Then he built a wigwam within the mountain and a fire in its center.

Geologists tell a different story about the mountain now called Mount Shasta. Volcanic activity that formed an ancestral mountain dates back about 600,000 years, they believe. This predecessor collapsed some 350,000 years ago. A series of eruptions formed today's Mount Shasta around 250,000 years ago, and an eruption 9,500 years ago formed Shastina to the west. The mountain's last eruption may have occurred in 1786, according to a French explorer who saw signs of it from his ship off the California coast.

Like the mountain, the name has changed over time too. Native Americans called it *Wyeka*, meaning "Great White," and *Bolempoiyok*, meaning "High Peak." A trapper named Peter Ogden encountered the Shasta Tribe in 1827, calling the people the Sastise and naming a large nearby mountain Mount Sastise. A mapmaker used the name Mount Shasty on an 1834 map, although researchers today believe both men were referring to the southern Oregon peak now called Mount McLoughlin. Though it had been called

---

MORE MOUNTAIN MATTERS

Mount Shasta marks the highest point of Siskiyou County.

This mountain combines elements of two kinds of volcanoes, qualifying as both a stratovolcano (composed of layers of lava flows, volcanic ash, cinders, and molten rocks) and also a composite volcano (consisting of multiple cones that overlap).

If you're looking for an alternative to Avalanche Gulch, consider Hotlum-Bolam Ridge on the north face of the mountain, which is longer but comparable in difficulty and far less populated.

Considering a winter ascent? Sargent's Ridge and Casaval Ridge are popular routes that avoid the avalanche hazard of the John Muir Route.

Alpenglow colors Mount Shasta at sunset.

both Mount Jackson and Pitt Mountain, a US government survey gave today's Mount Shasta its name in 1841.

Shasta, Modoc, Wintu, Karuk, Achumawi, and Atsugewi Tribes inhabited the area surrounding the mountain for thousands of years. Their oral history features Mount Shasta prominently. Life began here at a bubbling spring, according to folklore. Coyote once ran to the summit to escape a flood, though others met bad endings. An Indian god carried a beautiful maiden to his home on the summit, where she died of grief. Another maiden fled an arranged marriage with her preferred companion, Flying Eagle. But as they climbed Shasta's slopes in search of a new home, intense cold froze their blood and they perished. Such tales warn Indians not to climb the mountain, even though they revere it.

Although it's certainly possible that Native Americans climbed to the summit of Mount Shasta, a party of seven European Americans led by Elias Pearce made the first documented ascent in 1854. Three men made the first known winter ascent in 1856, despite an icy storm that inflicted frostbite severe enough to afflict them for decades. The first female ascent followed in September of 1856 by Harriet Eddy (some sources say Olive Eddy), Mary McCloud, Ann Lowry, Susan Gage, and Mary White.

Naturalist John Muir spotted Mount Shasta in 1874. "When I first caught sight of it, I was fifty miles away and afoot, alone and weary. Yet all my blood turned to wine, and I have not been weary since," claimed Muir, who climbed the mountain several times and survived an icy storm near the summit by huddling beside hot sulphur vents. Muir

According to legend, Bigfoots (Bigfeet?) occupy the mountain. They certainly inhabit the neighboring city.

played a key role in preserving the mountain and its surrounding wilderness, proposing a national park to encompass them in 1888. Others pursued that objective for decades without success.

However, President Teddy Roosevelt created Shasta and Trinity National Forests in 1905; the two eventually combined in 1954. The mountain became a national natural landmark in 1976, and Congress further protected 38,000 surrounding acres as wilderness in 1984.

The volcano has inspired countless writers and artists, including author Joaquin Miller who moved to its vicinity in 1854, penning admiring words, which made the volcano widely known. "Lonely as God, and white as a winter moon, Mount Shasta starts up sudden and solitary from the heart of the great black forests of Northern California," Miller wrote, also describing it as "the most comely and perfect snow peak in America." Arriving in 1917, Edward Stuhl admired and enjoyed Shasta for sixty-seven years and devoted a quarter-century to painting 204 species of wildflowers that grow upon its slopes. "I am certain Stuhl loved the mountain more than anyone, ever," wrote author Emilie Frank, who herself devoted twenty-five years to producing a book titled *Mt. Shasta: California's Mystic Mountain*.

Methodist pastor Douglas Smith endured three months at the summit to protest the Vietnam War in 1971. "As a dormant volcano, it was a natural peace symbol," he said. A Harmonic Convergence attracted thousands of similarly inspired believers to Shasta in 1987; they prayed for global peace while the planets were properly aligned.

More than any other mountain in the country, Shasta inspires myth and paranormal belief. Advanced beings called Lemurians inhabit a city within it. Survivors of Atlantis dwell in a city of their own. Dwarves reside in caves hidden inside it. Both UFOs and Bigfoot frequent the mountain, some claim.

Shasta's magnetic pull on climbers could be described as supernatural, too. Up to 10,000 climbers attempt the mountain per year, and about half of them reach the top, rangers estimate. Laurie Bagley broke the women's speed climbing record in 2005, ascending in 2 hours and 13 minutes. Ryan Ghelfi shattered the men's record in 2015, racing up in 1 hour and 37 minutes.

Four paraplegic climbers reached its summit in 2002. Blind mountaineer Erik Weihenmayer climbed Shasta and even skied down its west face in 2019. And Matthew and Arabella Adams, the five-year-old "Super Hiking Twins," became the youngest

A climber rests after an exhausting but successful ascent.

known climbers to reach the summit, with a little help from their parents, in 2020. "They couldn't wait to get to the top," said father Shaun Adams. "We are grateful that they enjoy the outdoors as much as we do."

MORE MOUNTAINS IN THE NORTH STATE

M. HERD PEAK

Distance: 0.1 mile round-trip (on-trail)
Time: Less than 1 hour
Difficulty: Class 1; easy
Land agency: Klamath National Forest
Nearest facilities: Weed
Trailhead elevation: 7,050 feet
Summit elevation: 7,071 feet
Elevation gain: 21 feet
Best season: May–Nov
Permits: None needed

Herd Peak

Visitors can drive within a stone's throw of this summit and its historic fire lookout in summer and fall. From Weed, take Highway 97 northeast for 19.8 miles. Turn left (northwest) on Forest Road 45N22. Drive 2.9 miles and then turn left at a Y onto 44N39Y. Drive 2.6 more miles to Herd Peak Lookout, constructed in 1933 and still staffed in summer. Winter visitors can ski or snowshoe 5.5 miles from Highway 97, gaining about 2,000 feet. Mountain biking is another option. Enjoy fine views of Goosenest, The Whaleback, Shasta Valley, and Mount Shasta.

N. GRAY BUTTE

Distance: 3.3 miles round-trip (all on trails)
Time: 2 to 3 hours
Difficulty: Class 1; easy
Land agency: Shasta-Trinity National Forest
Nearest facilities: Mount Shasta (city)
Trailhead elevation: 7,443 feet
Summit elevation: 8,108 feet
Elevation gain: 665 feet
Best season: June–Oct
Permits: None needed

Gray Butte

This short journey delivers a big mountain experience as it imparts an outstanding view of Mount Shasta and much more. Take Everitt Memorial Highway past Bunny Flat to Panther Meadow Campground. Gray Butte Trail leads east and turns south past red firs and mountain hemlocks. The trail curves clockwise to a summit known as Artist's Point, boasting an inspiring panorama of Mount Shasta, Lassen Peak, Castle Crags, and the Trinity Alps.

O. MOUNT BRADLEY

Distance: 11 miles round-trip (on trails and dirt roads)
Time: 4 to 6 hours
Difficulty: Class 1; moderate
Land agency: Shasta-Trinity National Forest
Nearest facilities: Dunsmuir
Trailhead elevation: 5,527 feet
Summit elevation: 5,556 feet
Elevation gain: 1,224 feet
Best season: May–Oct
Permits: None needed

Mount Bradley

The mountain's name honors Cornelius Bradley (1843–1936), a professor of rhetoric at the University of California. Civilian Conservation Corps workers built its lookout in 1933. Take Castle Lake Road (south of Mount Shasta and east of Interstate 5) to the trailhead at Castle Lake. Our trail winds its way east, traverses Mount Bradley Ridge, and joins a dirt road leading to the summit. A 7-mile dirt road from Dunsmuir to the peak provides another option for hikers, mountain bikers, or winter trekkers. Mount Eddy, Mount Shasta, and Castle Crags are a few of the peaks in view.

Sunset colors the sky above
Joshua Tree National Park.

AFTERWORD

I believe in positive thinking, but 2020 put that philosophy to the test. One year saw enough bad news to fill a decade. Wildfires broke records in California, racist violence set off nationwide protests, and COVID-19 ravaged the world. For many reasons, it seemed like the wrong time to climb mountains.

Yet I had signed a contract to produce the book in your hands by the end of the year, and I could not do that without several weeks of field work. So from my Bay Area home I traveled north, east, and south to ascend about twenty-five peaks, or half of this guide's fifty featured outings.

Scaling summits helped me escape heavy headlines. I enjoyed climbing with old friends Morry Angell on Mount Saint Helena and Paul Denzler on Granite Chief. Yosemite Sam the Samurai Dog accompanied me on Stanislaus Peak and many others. My brother Dan Johanson, his wife Hazel, and their children Nathan and Kaitlyn made a few family-friendly ascents with me, like Mount Davidson. My sister-in-law Galina Johanson climbed like a champ on her first-ever mountain, Jobs Peak. I loved hiking with my goddaughter Linnae Johansson on the Pacific Crest Trail for three days. Climbing Mount Diablo with my mom Diane Johanson, our first summit together, ranks as my favorite trek of the year.

Numerous challenges hindered my climbing spree, like hundreds of park closures to slow the spread of coronavirus. Luckily I was able to navigate them to hike atop Mount Sizer, Montara Mountain, Mount Tamalpais, and Tioga Peak. A surprise summer snowstorm and two flat tires impaired road trips I shared with my friend Bob Leung. We still managed to explore both Death Valley National Park and the North State, climbing Wildrose Peak, Cinder Cone, Granite Peak, and others.

By the time I drove south in August, wildfire and smoke had closed off my intended hike up San Gorgonio Mountain. Instead, I hiked with my friend David McPhee and his sons Kacen and Vincent up Echo Mountain. As the pandemic surged in summer, everyone wore masks to avoid infection on the narrow trail, a sight I had never before seen or expected. Even among the mountains, there was no escaping the year's hard news.

But while ball games, music concerts, and indoor dining disappeared as recreation options, millions of people who sheltered in place for months found relief outdoors. In fact, some summits from this book saw kindness and selfless heroism. Soccer coach Joe Owen didn't walk but ran up Mount Diablo (13 miles and 3,400 feet of climbing) every day in April to raise thousands of dollars for a local food bank. Members of Fremont High School's football team helped a wheelchair-bound climber reach the summit of Mission Peak in August. And thousands of firefighters risked life and limb to protect our forests and the public through the summer and fall.

What's more, California's outdoors became a little more welcoming as a revived civil rights movement led to a map makeover. A mountain, a giant sequoia, and a popular ski

Despite the pandemic, the Johanson family hiked to the summit of Mount Diablo.

area near Lake Tahoe all shed their racially insensitive names, with several other improvements pending elsewhere.

As I write these words in November 2020, no one can foresee the end of COVID-19 or California's annual wildfire ordeals. What I can do is offer you guidance and encouragement in climbing these summits in the hope that they lift you as they did me. If the outdoors provides a setting and inspiration for us to become our best selves, then maybe this is the best time to climb mountains. Happy trails.

High peaks and abundant sage typify Inyo National Forest.

HIKE INDEX

Black Butte, 221
Brokeoff Mountain, 237
Butler Peak, 75
Carson Peak, 185
Castle Dome, 229
Chocolate Mountain, 169
Cinder Cone, 217
Cuyamaca Peak, 79
Dante Peak, 204
Echo Mountain, 67
Ellis Peak, 152
Fremont Peak, 51
Gaylor Peak, 115
Goosenest, 213
Granite Chief, 135
Granite Peak, 241
Gray Butte, 258
Hawkins Peak, 31
Herd Peak, 258
Hiram Peak, 131
Jobs Peak, 139
Keller Peak, 103
Lassen Peak, 233
Little Baldy, 111
Lone Pine Peak, 195
Lookout Peak, 153
Matterhorn Peak, 199
Mission Peak, 27
Montecito Peak, 71
Mount Baden-Powell, 85
Mount Bradley, 259
Mount Davidson, 5
Mount Diablo, 9

Mount Eddy, 225
Mount Hollywood, 59
Mount Gould, 205
Mount Judah, 119
Mount Livermore, 50
Mount Montara, 21
Mount Saint Helena, 41
Mount San Antonio, 97
Mount Shasta, 251
Mount Sizer, 45
Mount Solomons, 177
Mount Starr, 181
Mount Tallac, 149
Mount Tamalpais, 17
Mount Umunhum, 37
North Dome, 127
Redwood Peak, 50
Reversed Peak, 161
Ryan Mountain, 63
San Bruno Mountain, 13
Sandstone Peak, 102
San Jacinto Peak, 93
Shastina, 247
Sierra Buttes, 152
Stanislaus Peak, 143
Tahquitz Peak, 89
Throop Peak, 102
Tioga Peak, 165
Trail Peak, 204
The Watchtower, 123
White Mountain, 189
Wildrose Peak, 173

ABOUT THE AUTHOR

Matt Johanson writes about the outdoors for numerous California newspapers and magazines. *California Summits* is his sixth book. Prior works include *Sierra Summits*, *Yosemite Adventures*, and *Yosemite Epics*. Matt's writing has won awards from the International Center for Journalists, California News Publishers Association, Outdoor Writers Association of California, and National Outdoor Book Awards Foundation. He lives in Castro Valley with his wife Karen.

THE TEN ESSENTIALS OF HIKING

American Hiking Society

American Hiking Society recommends you pack the "Ten Essentials" every time you head out for a hike. Whether you plan to be gone for a couple of hours or several months, make sure to pack these items. Become familiar with these items and know how to use them.

1. Appropriate Footwear
Happy feet make for pleasant hiking. Think about traction, support, and protection when selecting well-fitting shoes or boots.

2. Navigation
While phones and GPS units are handy, they aren't always reliable in the backcountry; consider carrying a paper map and compass as a backup and know how to use them.

3. Water (and a way to purify it)
As a guideline, plan for half a liter of water per hour in moderate temperatures/terrain. Carry enough water for your trip and know where and how to treat water while you're out on the trail.

4. Food
Pack calorie-dense foods to help fuel your hike, and carry an extra portion in case you are out longer than expected.

5. Rain Gear & Dry-Fast Layers
The weatherman is not always right. Dress in layers to adjust to changing weather and activity levels. Wear moisture-wicking cloths and carry a warm hat.

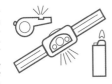

6. Safety Items (light, fire, and a whistle)
Have means to start an emergency fire, signal for help, and see the trail and your map in the dark.

7. First Aid Kit
Supplies to treat illness or injury are only as helpful as your knowledge of how to use them. Take a class to gain the skills needed to administer first aid and CPR.

8. Knife or Multi-Tool
With countless uses, a multi-tool can help with gear repair and first aid.

9. Sun Protection
Sunscreen, sunglasses, and sun-protective clothing should be used in every season regardless of temperature or cloud cover.

10. Shelter
Protection from the elements in the event you are injured or stranded is necessary. A lightweight, inexpensive space blanket is a great option.

Find other helpful resources at AmericanHiking.org/hiking-resources